VICTORIAN COTTAGES

ANDREW CLAYTON-PAYNE

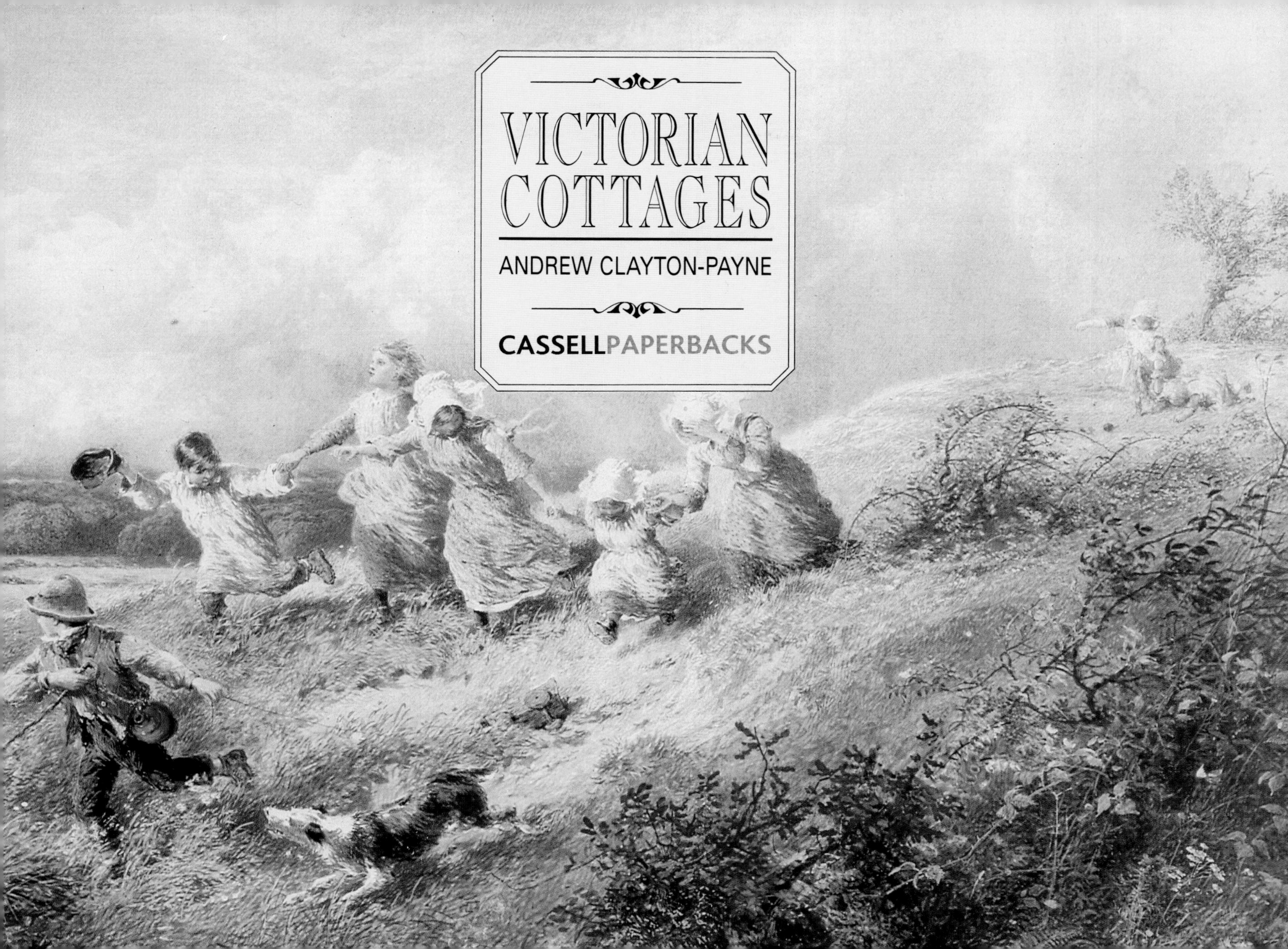
VICTORIAN
COTTAGES
ANDREW CLAYTON-PAYNE
CASSELLPAPERBACKS

for Camilla

First published in 1993 by George Weidenfeld & Nicolson Ltd

This paperback edition first published in 2002 by
Cassell Paperbacks, Cassell & Co
Wellington House, 125 Strand
London, WC2R 0BB

Distributed in the United States of America by
Sterling Publishing Co., Inc.
387 Park Avenue South,
New York, NY 10016-8810

British Library Cataloguing-in-Publication Data
A catalogue record for this book is available from
the British Library

ISBN 1-84188-176-7

Designer: Isobel Gillan
Phototypeset by Deltatype Ltd, Ellesmere Port, Cheshire
Colour separations by Newsele Litho Ltd
Printed and bound in Italy by L.E.G.O., Vicenza

Half-title page: The Visitor, Arthur Hopkins
Title page: Children Playing, Myles Birket Foster
Contents page: Near Haslemere, Helen Allingham
Opposite index: Vine Cottage, Helen Allingham

CONTENTS

Near Hambledon • *Helen Allingham*

INTRODUCTION

'I am glad to see you paint sunshine,' declared John Ruskin, the great nineteenth-century critic and arbiter of taste, after examining one of Helen Allingham's watercolours with his pocket-microscope. Later, he went on to praise her ability to represent 'the gesture, character and humour of charming children in a landscape'. After looking at the illustrations in this book, a sequence of carefree and happy country scenes, one may be forgiven for assuming that the cottage and its inhabitants existed in a Utopian vacuum. But did this rural paradise of cerulean skies, thatched roofs, rose-covered doorways and contented children really exist and why were artists so intent on capturing this way of life and making it one of the principle genres of Victorian art? Were artists simply mirroring a traditional way of country life, albeit in an idealized way, that existed at the end of the nineteenth century, or did they have a more serious, underlying intention?

To find out the answer to these questions it is necessary to understand how and why the cottage evolved in art and how people's attitudes and perceptions of it and its occupants have changed over the centuries. Today, the cottage is often regarded as being the second home of city dwellers, an anachronistic bolthole to escape to at weekends, a place that exudes rustic charm but with the modern amenities of the twentieth century. The cottage during Queen Victoria's reign was regarded somewhat differently.

The British, more than any other European nation, have always been fascinated by houses, perhaps a reflection on both the status they attach to them and their unpredictable climate. A brief survey of British art soon reveals this special, almost obsessive relationship between house and owner. In the seventeenth century, only the grandest country houses were portrayed, giving the owner a visual record of his wealth and standing in society, such as in Jan Siberecht's famous aerial view of Longleat painted in 1675. But it was not until the second half of the eighteenth century that the more humble cottage was considered worthy of inclusion as the main subject in an artist's work. In the 1770s Thomas Gainsborough, one of England's greatest painters, began to introduce the cottage into his landscapes, often with peasants at the cottage door, where they became symbols of rural simplicity and acted as a natural, if not moral, adjunct to the landscape. Sir Uvedale Price, the Picturesque theorist, observed about him in *Essay on the Picturesque* (1794) that he was 'at times severe and sarcastic but', he continues, 'when he came to cottage or village scenes, to groups of children, or to any objects of that kind which struck his fancy, I have often remarked in his countenance an expression of particular gentleness and complacency'. Other artists, such as George Morland, working at the same time, depicted cottages but in a more sentimental way. Perhaps it was the influence of William Gilpin, another Picturesque theorist, which discouraged more artists in the eighteenth century from using the cottage as a motif. 'Nothing can reconcile me to a cottage. In nature it pleases me . . . but when I see it in a picture, I always remove my eye . . . I can give no reason, why a cottage may not make a pleasing picture. All I can say, is, that my eye is so captivated with sublime objects, that it will bear no other.'

For centuries the cottage and its inhabitants had been the focus of much intellectual debate for they represented different things to different people. For instance, as early as 1775 Nathanial Kent wrote in *Hints to Gentlemen of Landed Property*: 'The shattered hovels which half the poor of this kingdom are obliged to put up with, is truly affecting to a heart fraught with humanity. Those who condescend to visit these miserable tenements can testify that neither health or decency can be preserved in them.' However, William Paley writing only a few years later about the condition of the rustic labourer in *Reasons for Contentment Addressed to the Labouring Part of the British Public* (1792) saw their existence from a rather different angle: 'if the face of happiness can anywhere be seen, it is in the summer evening of a country village; where, after the labours of the day, each man at his door, with his children, amongst his neighbours, feels his frame and his heart at rest, every thing about him pleased and pleasing, and a delight and a complacency in his sensations far beyond what either luxury or diversion can afford'. The two divergent attitudes can be summed up by, on the one hand, those who believed the cottagers were to be pitied for their poverty and desperate lives spent in miserable surroundings, or on the other, to be envied for their attainment of dignity and happiness through their simple abodes and honest labour.

The Romantic movement erupted in the early part of the nineteenth century with artists such as John Constable, Joseph Mallord William Turner, David Cox and Peter de Wint. Their response to nature was a highly subjective and imaginative one, and cottages and cottage life became an integral part of an emotionally perceived landscape. They were seen both as symbolic of a traditional way of life and as a device through which to make an emotional social comment on issues such as enclosure.

By the second half of the nineteenth century the full impact of the Industrial Revolution was beginning to be felt across the country with disastrous effects for the cottage and the traditional way of life. The greater part of the agricultural workforce had fled the countryside to find work in the factories and mills of the emergent industrial cities such as Manchester and Sheffield leaving behind not only their homes but their customs as well. The railways lacerated the countryside which encouraged greater movement of people and soon nowhere was more than a few hours away. The nightmare scenario of Charles Dickens's Coketown had become a reality by the 1870s with England changing almost overnight from an agricultural to an industrial based economy. He writes in *Hard Times* (1854) of the universal consequences: 'Time went on in Coketown like its own machinery . . . the piston of the steam-engine worked monotonously up and down like the head of an elephant in a state of melancholy madness . . . Their wearisome heads went up and down at the same rate, in hot weather and cold, wet weather and dry, fair weather and foul. The measured motion of their shadows on the walls, was the substitute Coketown had to show for the shadows of rustling woods; while, for the summer hum of insects, it could offer, all the year round . . . the whirr of shafts and wheels.'

It was not until the last thirty years of the nineteenth century when the machine age was well underway that cottages and cottage life were so visually well-documented. At this time artists were diversifying their interests and specializing in different genres and the 1870s and 1880s saw a group of them focusing particularly on this theme. The social realists were intent on showing the desperate lives of poor rustics living in 'the shattered hovels' while the cottage artists wanted to represent 'the face of happiness'. They were responding in part to a middle-class demand for nostalgic views of a country way of life which had been threatened by the Industrial Revolution but were also motivated by their own personal concerns for the conservation of the cottages themselves.

The two artists most closely associated with Victorian cottage painting are Myles Birket Foster and Helen Allingham; both were highly thought of by their contemporaries and they influenced a whole generation of artists from Arthur Claude Strachan and Charles Edward Wilson to Thomas Mackay and David Woodlock. They both moved to Witley in Surrey where a circle of artists soon settled inspired by their example and the cottage theme. Not only were the artists concerned about the disappearance of a country way of life but they were also aware that cottages were being ruined or destroyed by insensitive restoration and by the demand for new houses by people living in the suburbs of large towns and cities which were encroaching upon nearby hamlets and villages. In 1877 William Morris, who helped design the interior of Birket Foster's house, The Hill, at Witley, created The Society for Protection of Ancient Buildings and how serious a matter the situation had become is nicely summarized by William Allingham, Helen's husband, in his preface to the catalogue of her exhibition, Surrey Cottages, held in 1886. He writes: 'in the short time, to be counted by months, since these drawings were made, no few of the Surrey Cottages, which they represent have been thoroughly "done up" and some of them swept away'.

A criticism which is often levelled at Helen Allingham and Myles Birket Foster is that they indulged in nostalgic frivolity and presented a superficial and simplistic view of life at the expense of truth. As there are a number of lesser known watercolours by Birket Foster and Allingham which depict dismal scenes of poverty and falling-down cottages, they were, however, quite clearly well aware of the reality.

As Allingham's desire to draw attention to the speed with which life and cottages in the country were being destroyed by creeping urbanization grew, so her pictures became more idealized, less varied and less truthful. Her cottages took on an air of uniformity as doors, windows and unsightly chimneys were moved

Cottage at Dusk • *Myles Birket Foster*

to more convenient positions and beautiful models, painted later in the studio, were employed to replace the weather-worn faces of the washerwoman or milkmaid. However, the manipulation of the real world must have been accepted, and to a great extent demanded, by her buying public. A justification of her approach was given by A. L. Baldry who wrote in *The Practice of Watercolour Painting* (1911): 'Her method of painting is to copy with all fidelity what is before her, or rather, so much of what is before her as she wishes to represent. Anything that jars or that is out of harmony with her pictorial intention she leaves out, and the resulting gaps in her composition are filled up with appropriate material gathered elsewhere . . . it leads to entirely acceptable results and it conveys a true impression of natural beauty.' There is no doubt that for Allingham this method of working achieved her dual objectives of creating a commercial image at the same time as making people aware of what was happening to the countryside.

Myles Birket Foster also tended towards a nostalgic view but for him people, especially children, were the important part of a picture rather than the cottage which acts as a backcloth. Figures for him are active and are rarely seen standing idly by the cottage gate. He was interested in recording life as he saw it but, like Allingham, with a veneer of commercial respectability, so pedlars and chair-menders are often models worked up later in the studio. Nevertheless, there is always a real concern about the rapidity with which life was changing and his pictures are imbued with a feeling that traditional life will never again be the same.

The lack of variety in the cottage artist's subject matter must be accounted for by the practical reason that their formula found enormous popularity among the new-rich middle classes living in the cities who wished to have an escapist country scene. When Birket Foster died in 1899 he left over thirty thousand pounds, a substantial sum in those days, and after the death of her husband William in 1889 Allingham supported her family from the sale of her pictures.

Perhaps a literary parallel to the work and aims of the cottage artists can be found in the work of a Surrey neighbour Gertrude Jekyll who, in the Introduction to her book *Old English Household Life* (1925), laments the price paid for progress. 'The last sixty years have seen so many changes in the ways of living among the rural working people of the country, that it is well to have some written remembrance of the older, and in many respects, better ways that are within the memory of people still living . . . Their way of living and outlook on life had gone on almost unchanged for generations, and, except when specially hard times came, as in the forties of the nineteenth century, they were happy and content.'

Stannard, Strachan and Wilson are among the second generation of cottage artists to continue the cottage genre in to the first decades of this century but it was not until the appearance of a third generation of cottage artists such as David Woodlock and Thomas Mackay that the traditional techniques and palette gave way to the more adventurous ideas absorbed from their contemporaries in Europe. The cottage is depicted but its importance becomes secondary to the symphony of colours and abstract patterns created across the paper.

The popularity of the cottage genre a hundred years after its golden period echoes our present day concerns with conserving our environment and the cottage has once again come to represent a vital part of our heritage.

Old Surrey Cottage • *Helen Allingham*

CHAPTER ONE

TRADITIONAL COUNTRY COTTAGES

Throughout history the much loved English cottage has meant different things to different people and to a certain extent it has become a victim of its own image. The proof of this is that it is almost impossible to give an accurate definition of a cottage. Is it a farm labourer's small thatched house set on its own in rolling green hills or is it something larger like Jane Austen's Barton Cottage in *Sense and Sensibility* (1811) which had four large bedrooms, two sitting rooms and enough accommodation for servants, or is it a picturesque folly built for people of 'refined manners and habits' as W. F. Pocock refers to it in *Architectural Designs for Rustic Cottages* (1807). Perhaps it is the fact that the cottage was created out of necessity and has continued to evolve over the centuries that makes it defy categorization; the cottage is not and never has been a static building but one that is constantly changing either because of the organic materials used, like thatch, or because the original purpose has changed. In England there are over fifty thousand cottages and however hard one may struggle to come up with a definition, the cottage still remains the most evocative image of the English countryside.

Originally, the main purpose of a cottage was to give protection against unfavourable weather conditions. Over the centuries, the cottage evolved from being little more than a poorly constructed hut to something more substantial and permanent. By the fifteenth century, a tradition of building cottages had been established and the majority of the cottages shown in this book were built after this date. At that time, builders had no pattern books to refer to but instead the use of materials, ideas and techniques were passed down by word of mouth, which is why styles are so particular to certain localities.

The earliest cottages were constructed of mud, or cob as it is called in Devon, because it was easy to use and the unskilled cottager could make it himself. By the fifteenth century, timber was being more widely used because of the accessibility of many thousands of acres of woodland and because of the development of building techniques. The cruck frame, which consists of two pairs of large timbers fixed in the ground and bent inwards to meet at the top and connected by a ridge pole, was one of the earliest forms of timber construction (few examples of this survive today). This was succeeded by the box frame, that is, a box shape made with horizontal and vertical timbers which are infilled with wattle and daub or brick. These are still seen in many parts of the country but most characteristically in Surrey, Kent and Sussex.

Cottages made from stone are among the most beautiful and natural in England. The great advantage of stone is that it does not rot and disintegrate, which in time made it a more favourable building material than wood. However, the inherent disadvantages of stone for the cottager were its cost (most stone walls were about two feet deep), it was expensive to cut and it was cold and damp in winter. The complex geological structure of England means that types of stone vary depending on the area, which is why cottages made of limestone are prevalent in the Cotswolds, granite ones in Northumberland and flint ones in Norfolk. The variety of stone and its colour give whole areas their special character. However, with the improvements in transport in the nineteenth century stone was moved over greater distances and henceforth buildings were no longer necessarily made from the indigenous materials of the area.

Like stone, brick was more expensive than timber and was not widely used before it was mass-produced in the nineteenth century, but even then it was subject to a Brick Tax introduced in 1784 and not repealed until 1850. Its high cost also accounts for many cottages only being part built in brick, the rest being made from other less expensive materials. The colour of brick depended on the clay in the area and there were local traditions of arranging bricks in different ways to create decorative effects such as the herring-bone pattern.

Once the basic structure of the building had been completed, whether it was made of mud, wood, stone or brick or a combination of any of these, the next most important part of the building was the roof. This was made of either thatch, slate or clay tiles. For many people, a cottage is not a cottage without a picture postcard thatched roof and, traditionally, most cottages had some form of thatch. However, the disadvantage of thatch was that it was always a fire risk and even though it could last for a long time it was difficult and expensive to repair if it became damaged. The dwindling numbers of thatchers towards the end of the last century shows the popularity of other roofing materials such as clay tiles, either plain tiles or curved pantiles, or slate. Both of these materials were heavier than thatch and roofs had to be strengthened to bear the extra weight. Unlike thatch, the regular shape of tiles meant that roofs could no longer be shaped around garret windows which meant that the curved and irregular lines of the traditional thatched roof gave way to distinct, symmetrical ones. Ironically, for the cottage artist who is associated with thatched roofs, tiled roofs were often more interesting to paint because of the different colours and the textural effects created by moss and lichen which grew over them. Tiles were also hung on the walls of cottages to help insulate them and the decorative effects achieved by using different fan-shaped tiles are typical of cottages in Surrey and Kent.

Poorly insulated walls, draughty windows and badly made doors inevitably meant that the fireplace was the centre of life inside the cottage. Here was the source of heat and also the main source of light as rushlights (peeled rushes dipped in grease) were often inadequate and candles and paraffin lamps were too expensive for many cottagers. If there was no cast-iron range, something which was quite a luxury for most cottagers, then the cooking was done in a pot over the open fire. In earlier cottages the fireplace and chimney are placed in the centre of the cottage which meant that the heat would radiate out from the chimney stack as it went up through the cottage, but the disadvantage of this was that it reduced the amount of room upstairs which is why many chimney stacks were moved to the gable end.

Running water in a cottage is a comparatively recent introduction. At the end of the last century and for the first few decades of this, water was collected from a well or a running brook. If the cottage did not have its own well then water was carried over long distances in heavy earthenware jars and often the temptation to use water from a nearby stagnant pond was too much to resist. Little was then known of diseases such as typhoid which is carried in unclean water, and whole families and communities were sometimes decimated by using dirty water. Disease was also spread by the lack of sanitation and the garden was often considered the best place to dispose of refuse and sewage.

Most of the interiors illustrated in this book show clean, homely and well-ordered cottage interiors which to a great extent mirror Flora Thompson's memoir of cottage life in *Lark Rise* in Oxfordshire in the 1880s where she describes the interiors as being 'kept clean by much scrubbing with soap and water' and that they were 'bright and cosy, with dressers of crockery, cushioned chairs and pictures on the wall'. In fact, very much how we would expect to find the inside of a country cottage today. However, judging from the evidence of contemporary reports the interiors she was familiar with were not typical. This is confirmed by the number of commissions set up in the latter half of the nineteenth century to expose the horrors of cottage and rural life. Richard Heath in his contemporary view of rural life in the 1870s writes: 'Picturesque and harmonious from the artist's point of view these cottages are in most other respects a scandal to England . . .' He then goes on to quote from a report made by the Reverend James Fraser for the commission on the employment of children in agriculture (1867): 'the majority of cottages that exist in rural parishes are deficient in almost every requisite that should constitute a home for a Christian family in a civilised community. They are deficient in bedroom accommodation . . . They are deficient in drainage and sanitary arrangements . . . they are so full of draughts to generate any amount of rheumatism; and in many instances are lamentably delapidated and out of repair. It is almost impossible to exaggerate the ill effects such a state of things in every aspect, physical, social, economical, moral, intellectual . . . The moral consequences are fearful to contemplate . . . Modesty must be an unknown virtue, decency an unimaginable thing, where in one small chamber . . . two and sometimes three generations are herded promiscuously . . . where the whole atmosphere is sensual, and human nature is degraded into something below the level of the swine. It is a hideous picture, and the picture is drawn from life.' Reports such as these suggest that for the majority of cottagers their rose-bedecked cottages, with perfectly manicured thatch roofs, hid a desperately miserable interior and that for the Victorian commissioners it was the spectre of moral corruption caused by overcrowding which concerned them as much as the cottagers' physical discomfort.

Figures outside a Cottage • *Helen Allingham*

As explained, the cottage evolved entirely out of a local building tradition and the economic constraints of the rural community, but at the end of the eighteenth century, with the fashion for the Picturesque, writers and architects started to turn their attention to ways of recreating the rustic cottages observed in the country by writing pattern books, a source of ideas for architects and builders, thereby altering the whole concept of the cottage. Following Sir Uvedale Price's *Essay on the Picturesque* (1794), James Malton wrote *Essay on British Cottage Architecture* (1798) which describes how cottages must be, above all else, irregular and must look pleasing on a gentleman's estate. Little attention was given to the inside of the cottage and the comfort of the inhabitants for it was the impression given to the passer-by which was important. Other designs could be found in a plethora of similar publications. The fashion for cottages was taken one stage further with the advent of the *cottage orné*, a term used to describe a romantic and often eccentric cottage retreat for the rich built at seaside resorts like Brighton and Sidmouth. The rage for these resulted in some of the country's most original and eccentric architectural creations. Cottages were no longer seen exclusively as the rural abode of the poor, but rather as experimental follies for the rich to admire and, on occasion, to live in. Styles and influences were multifarious but the result was always unique. A *cottage orné* could be anything from a miniature thatched castle to a Swiss chalet, such as the one at Osborne on the Isle of Wight. At the beginning of the nineteenth century, they captured the imagination of artists but by the second half, after a cottage genre had been established, their originality was shunned by artists in favour of the traditional country cottage.

Apart from isolated cottages in remote areas, cottages were either in or near a village or hamlet. Most villages evolved gradually over centuries catering for the social and economic needs of the inhabitants and surrounding area. Until transport became easier with the increase in the number of railways and the improvements in roads, villages were to a large extent unaffected by the outside world and were able to retain their own identity and character. The change in this relationship from the 1880s onwards altered the whole nature of village life and soon the prosperous middle-classes began to invade the countryside at weekends looking for a rural way of life that had already changed.

Running parallel to the natural development of the traditional village was the appearance of the model village, a concept which dates back to the eighteenth century. After the fashion for the excesses of the

Picturesque had subsided, the original desire to give workers a decent home with proper facilities became widely popular in the nineteenth century and resulted in purpose-built villages, like Port Sunlight in Cheshire, which went a long way to improve rural and industrial workers' living conditions.

Most of the cottages in this book had their origins in the fifteenth, sixteenth and seventeenth centuries but they continued to evolve and develop. A cottager who was able to, would add a bread oven, or put in an extra window or door, and just as the cottages would have changed from the time they were built to the time they were painted by the Victorian artists, so many have changed since then. One of the major concerns of the cottage artists was the number of cottages being pulled down in their lifetime, and it is encouraging that one can still find many of the cottages depicted in the paintings in this book still standing today.

Fowl House Farm • *Myles Birket Foster*

For centuries, the most common material used for building cottages was wood. It was easily obtainable (it has been estimated that at the end of the seventeenth century there were over three million acres of woods in England), relatively simple to construct with and cheaper than other materials such as brick. Oak was most widely favoured as it was harder and longer lasting than other types, such as elm and willow, and it was also thought to improve with age.

There were two main types of timber construction: cruck and box frame. The main feature of a cruck-framed building is the A shape which is created by large timbers fixed in the ground (traditionally, about fifteen feet apart, a measurement based on the width of a team of four oxen harnessed together) which are curved inwards and joined at the apex as shown in the picture on the right. These are then interlinked by a ridge pole which runs the length of the building. In effect, there is no differentiation between the roof and the walls. This was the earliest form of construction which was superseded by the box frame which is seen on the left. The roofs are raftered and rest on a framework of upright posts and horizontal beams forming the box frame which we are familiar with today in counties like Surrey, Kent and Sussex. Various materials could be used to fill the spaces between the timbers, the most popular being wattle and daub or brick.

Cruck Cottage • *Helen Allingham*

Bourton-on-the-Hill, Gloucestershire • *Arthur Claude Strachan*

Stone cottages, more than any other type of cottage, blend most naturally with their environment, a fact which Wordsworth commented on: 'These humble dwellings remind the spectator of a production of nature and rather may be said to have grown than to have been created; to have risen, by an instinct of their own, out of naked rock.'

The type of stone used would vary from granite cottages on Dartmoor to sandstone in Yorkshire and flint in Norfolk, mirroring the local geology and giving each area its special character. Stone cottages, however, often proved to be the coldest and dampest to live in because the stones for the outside walls and the flagstones for the floors were often placed directly onto the ground without any foundation, which would draw up the water. The illustration on the right is typical of a Welsh cottage built from rough boulders found in the vicinity. It is unlikely that mortar would have been used to infill the spaces and often mud would have been pushed between giving only a poor protection against the elements. This cottage with its tiny windows would have been very dark and gloomy inside, even on a summer's day. The cottage belonged to the famous early-nineteenth-century watercolourist David Cox.

An example of a more refined stone cottage is the one illustrated to the left. It is from the Cotswolds in Gloucestershire and made of limestone which is found only a few feet below the ground. It is easily cut as it is softer than many other stones but it hardens when exposed to the weather for any period of time. Its subtle faded yellow colour gives the whole region its character. Cotswold cottages would not normally have been thatched, but would have had roofs of local slate instead.

David Cox's Cottage, Bettws-y-Coed • *Myles Birket Foster*

Country Cottages • *Ralph William Bardell*

Surprisingly, many cottages hidden behind a layer of whitewash are not made of stone, as one would expect, but of hardened earth or mud. Cottages of this type are found throughout Devon, Dorset, parts of Somerset and some areas in East Anglia and the Midlands. Earth, or cob as it is called in Devon (or wychert in Buckinghamshire), which has not been fired has been a popular material since earliest times because it is both easy to use and always readily available. Also, one did not need to employ skilled craftsmen as construction was fairly basic and often the cottager himself would build his own house.

The earth would be dug from the ground and then mixed with water to make it malleable and straw or animal hair was added for strengthening. Stones and other impurities would be extracted before it was trodden down until the right consistency was reached. It was then laid, usually not more than two feet at a time, and compacted down by walking on it (Thomas Hardy in a letter to *The Times* wrote, 'women were sometimes called in to tread'). The walls were made to a depth of between two and three feet which was both thick enough to keep the heat in and the wet weather out. An alternative method of making the walls was to form the earth into brick shapes. Called clay lump, this was probably used to avoid paying the Brick Tax which was introduced in 1784.

The nature of the material and the use of unskilled labour accounts for the rounded walls and their charmingly amateur appearance. Once the walls had been built the windows were cut out and then the earth was left to dry for up to a year. A brick chimney stack was then added and a thatched roof; tiles were too heavy. The thatch would overhang the walls to protect them from the rain, as without modern downpipes and gutters the walls would get soaked and this would lead to their eventual decay.

At Symondsbury near Bridport, Dorset • *Helen Allingham*

Cottages at Wheeler Street, Witley • *Myles Birket Foster*

The Faggot Gatherer's Meal • *William Henry Hunt*

The great advantage of using brick as a building material, as opposed to wood, is its fire resistant qualities.

Before bricks were mass-produced in the nineteenth century, they were made from local earth and clay which was trodden on to extract any impurities such as pebbles or pieces of wood. The earth was then smoothed into wooden moulds which were left to dry in a covered place. They were then placed in a makeshift kiln by the side of the cottage. Inconsistent control of the kiln's temperature often resulted in different shaped and textured bricks but their 'hand-made' appearance added to the charm of the cottage.

The colour of brick varied from area to area depending on certain elements in the clay – clay rich in iron would have a deep, rich, red hue while a clay with more lime would have a light brown appearance. The decorative effects of brickwork could be enhanced by the use of different coloured bricks and by arranging them in different patterns. On some cottages, for aesthetic as well as insulation reasons, the brickwork would be plastered and over a period of time damp would force its way behind this causing some of it to crumble, leaving an unintentionally appealing textural effect.

The picture above shows the inside of a faggot gatherer's cottage. The brickwork would have afforded little insulation. The one on the left shows a cottage which was demolished soon after this picture was painted. Wheeler Street ran from Milford to Witley.

A Highland Cottage • *Myles Birket Foster*

Highland cottages such as these are markedly different to their counterparts in southern England, both in construction and their impoverished appearance. They were built using the most basic materials. The walls were of local stone and probably had no infilling, making the cottages cold, and damp. The living area inside would have been restricted, probably to only one or two rooms, and these were sometimes shared with animals. The absence of a chimney stack in either of these pictures suggests that the fire was still being lit on the floor.

The thatch was usually made of heather and the unsuitability of this illustrates to what extent crofters' life styles depended on the whim of the estate owner. Sir Dick Lauder gave an absurd example when he edited Sir Uvedale Price's influential book *Essay on the Picturesque* (1794): 'I remember a highland proprietor, a friend of mine, who has constructed in different parts of his grounds, some of the most picturesque cottages I ever beheld which were all thatched with heather. When I first saw them, I was loud in my praise of his good taste, and high in my praise of fine heather thatch. "It is very beautiful indeed" said he to me. "It has but one fault indeed, and that is that it does not keep out one drop of rain". Now I do not think that anyone has the right to make his cottagers suffer to such an extent as this in order that their cottages may look picturesque to his friends as they drive past them in an open carriage on a sunshiny day.'

A Cottage in the Trossachs • *Myles Birket Foster*

The Thatcher • *Henry John Sylvester Stannard*

It is difficult to imagine a typically English landscape without a thatched cottage nestling somewhere in it and, indeed, to many the very idea of thatch sums up the English countryside. The word derives from 'thack' which used to mean any roof covering but with the introduction of more modern materials such as tiles it came to refer to only organic materials like reed or straw. The thatcher seen working in the watercolour above would have had a large number of different materials to choose from, depending on which part of the country he worked in. For instance, reed was widely used around Norfolk and Suffolk because of its ready availability from the marshes and rivers, whereas a material such as heather would have been extensively used in a county like Devon where it grew in abundance on the moors. Reed was the preferred material, even though it was comparatively expensive, because it could last for as long as eighty years with minimum maintenance while less weather hardy materials sometimes needed replacing after only twenty-five years. The main disadvantage of thatch was that the slightest spark on a summer's day could set the whole cottage alight which is why, at one time, many had lime plaster applied over the top to reduce the risk. Also, thatch was difficult to repair without employing a professional thatcher and it offered an ideal home to birds and vermin. Many Victorian cottagers therefore replaced their thatch with more practical materials such as clay tiles, but as this was more expensive than thatch it tends to be only the more substantial cottages which have them.

Happy Moments • *Henry John Sylvester Stannard*

Near Witley, Surrey • *Helen Allingham*

In 1904 Gertrude Jekyll commented in her book *Old West Surrey* that by the 1890s thatching was 'almost extinct as a way of roofing'. Contemporary records from the 1880s to the early part of this century confirm that thatchers were dwindling in numbers while more people were being employed as tilers. Both the pictures illustrated here show cottages with beautifully coloured roofs of tiles, roofs which would have been thatched before the introduction of low cost tiles during the nineteenth century. However, these cottages would not have belonged to poor labourers as even with the mass production of tiles it was still cheaper to thatch. Also, the structure of the building would have to be quite sturdy to take the heavier weight of tiles. The two main types of tiles used were plain tiles and pantiles. Plain tiles became the most common alternative to thatch and many cottages throughout England and especially in the south-east still have them. They are made of clay and baked in a large kiln, the colour of them depending on the colour of the clay found in that area. For instance, colours can vary from honey yellow in Cambridgeshire to various shades of red ranging from terracotta to a faded pink in Kent and Surrey. Pantiles (curved roof tiles) became popular because of their interesting shape and also, because of their design, less were needed making them both lighter to use and more economical. But the disadvantage of pantiles was that they were not suitable for very steep roofs or for tiling around unusual features, like dormer windows. They appear most often on cottages built on the east or north-east coast of England because they were originally imported from Holland where they were first made.

In the picture on the right the ivy has grown rampant over the cottage, obscuring part of the roof and all of the chimney. The picture on the left has moss and lichen growing on the tiles which give a colourful and soft textural effect to the roof.

At Stedham near Midhurst • *Helen Allingham*

Outside the Cottage • *Charles Edward Wilson*

In medieval cottages, the principal function of windows or 'wind-eyes', as they were known, was to let smoke escape (as there would have been no chimney) and these were often placed as high as possible; it was only later that they were used to let light in. The problem facing most householders was how to have an opening which allowed light to enter but kept the weather out. Glass was difficult to make and expensive to buy, and even as late as the early part of the nineteenth century most cottage windows were unglazed. In its place sometimes thin slivers of horn were used but most popular of all was oiled cloth stretched across an opening.

The windows set in to the end wall of the cottage illustrated on the left show an unusual combination of diamond-shaped panes divided by lead supports and next to it a window with rectangular panes divided by upright and horizontal bars of wood. The most common type of glass was cylinder glass which tended to be rough and not very clear. This was superseded by a better quality glass called crown glass which is still often seen in cottages. In the middle of the nineteenth century, sheet glass was introduced which was both cheaper and easier to use. Shutters, as seen in the watercolour on the right, often appeared on the outside of cottages and were an important device for keeping out the wind and rain as most windows were poorly made and gaping holes were left between the frame and the glass. They were usually made of horizontal planks of wood hinged at the side, as here, but on timber-framed cottages they usually slid from side to side. Some cottages had windows blocked up as a result of the controversial Window Tax which was first introduced in 1696 and was not repealed until 1851.

A Moment's Rest • *Thomas Mackay*

Outside the Cottage • *Myles Birket Foster*

The Victorian cottager faced a constant battle against the elements. Cottages were draughty, cold and damp and an effective method of weatherproofing the exterior walls was to hang them with tiles. The use of tiles in this way is known to have existed as early as the seventeenth century but it became most popular at the end of the nineteenth century when cheaper machine-made tiles became widely available and more affordable. Originally, hand-made plain tiles would have been used to cover the walls of timber-framed cottages and most villages in Kent, Sussex and Surrey have examples of this. They were also used for the very pragmatic reason that they were not taxed like bricks and so only the bottom half of a cottage would be bricked and the rest tile-hung. Apart from practical considerations, tile-hung cottages were also more attractive, especially when different shapes of tiles were used rather than the standard rectangular ones. A feature of the cottages illustrated here is the 'fish scale' shaped tiles which were often combined with other shapes, such as diamond or herring-bone; different coloured tiles caused by the colour of the local clay also enhanced the decorative effect. Sometimes, tiles which looked identical to bricks were used not only to beat the Brick Tax but also as a convenient and inexpensive way of modernizing an old timber-framed house.

A Cottage at Haslemere • *Helen Allingham*

The Pet Kid • *Charles Edward Wilson*

A Village Street, Kent • *Helen Allingham*

To fill the empty areas between the studs (the vertical posts of a cottage frame) different materials were employed. Slabs of stone were sometimes used but the most common filler was wattle and daub. The daub (mud or clay mixed with straw or something of similar texture) would be fixed around the wattle which was made up of long, thin pieces of wood fitted vertically and horizontally between the studs. Later, when bricks became less expensive due to the mass production of them and the abolition of the Brick Tax in 1850, they were inserted in the place of daub and wattle and this became known as brick nogging. Often, they were used to form decorative designs by being arranged in a herring-bone formation. The disadvantage of this type of infilling was that it tended to be quite thin and often did not fit in between the studs very well and as a result let in damp and rain and let out heat. The solution to this problem was to clad the outside of the walls. Plaster was commonly used and spread over the interior and exterior of the building and motifs were sometimes incised into the plaster in decorative shapes such as fans or scallops. This technique was called pargetting.

A more economical way of weatherproofing a cottage was to clad it with weatherboards which are long planks of wood attached to the outside of the house, as shown in the centre of this line of cottages in the watercolour above. Such examples can still be seen today in counties such as Kent and Surrey. This method was widely emulated in America on the 'clapper board' houses of New England.

The Young Angler • *Charles Edward Wilson*

From the outside, the chimney is one of the most distinctive features of a Victorian cottage, adding a strong vertical accent to the building to counteract the strong horizontal line of the roof. Originally, most of the cottages we see today would not have had a chimney for the fire was lit in the centre of the floor and the smoke escaped through an open window or door. With the introduction of chimneys the quality of life rapidly improved as people no longer had to endure a smoke-filled, soot-encrusted room. However, early chimneys were invariably made of the wrong materials, such as wattle and daub or even wood, and as a result often caught fire. This led to a decree in London in the fifteenth century 'that henceforth no chimney shall be made except it be of stone, tiles, or brick and not of plaster or wood under pain of being pulled down'.

At first, brick chimneys were placed in the centre of the cottage (known as the axial stack) which was useful for heating purposes but being placed centrally as in the picture on the right made an awkward division and reduced the amount of living space especially upstairs. Later, chimney stacks were added at the gable ends of the cottage as in the picture on the left. The advantage of this was that a large bread oven could be added on to the base of the stack, a feature which was considered a luxury; in poor villages there would sometimes only be one such oven. Also, once the chimney had been removed from the central position, there was more living space created within the cottage.

As chimneys were such a prominent feature it was not unheard of for the artist painting a particular cottage to use artistic licence and move them to a more picturesque position. Chimneypots, which vary enormously in shape and size, were first introduced at the end of the eighteenth century but were not widely used on cottages such as these until some fifty years later.

A Thatched Cottage • *Arthur Claude Strachan*

A Cottage Interior • *Francis Berry-Berry*

Cottage life tended to be centred around the fireplace. It was here that on a cold winter's evening the inhabitants would gather to keep warm. Also, for many who could not afford rushlights or candles it was the only form of light on a dark evening. The fireplaces were usually very large, often with enough room for several people to sit inside, with a wide hearth so that awkward shaped logs and branches could be easily accommodated. They were placed directly on to the hearth or on fire dogs which raised the wood so that a draught could circulate underneath and encourage the wood to burn. In the watercolour on the right the young boy is looking after an old iron pot in which most of the cooking was done. These were either supported on a tripod or suspended from a chimney-crane. The old-fashioned kettle would also hang from the crane and this was tilted forward by using an 'idle-back'. Other useful instruments found in and around the fireplace were bellows, roasting spits, brand-tongs and baking irons.

In the picture on the left the heavy brick chimney stack is supported by a sturdy oak lintel which characteristically had a decorative piece of cloth hanging from it. In the picture on the right we can see a back oven which was used if the cottage did not have a separate baking oven. A more well-to-do cottager would replace the fireplace with a cast-iron range which was more convenient and took up less room. Richard Heath, the chronicler of late Victorian country life, wrote about the fireplace in a way which gives a less romantic idea of the cottage hearth than shown in these two pictures. Describing the interior of a cob cottage in Dorset, he writes: 'There is no grate, but a huge open chimney, with a few bricks upon the hearth, on which the miserable inhabitants place their fuel – sometimes nothing but clods of peat, emitting wretched acrid vapours. Owing to the low open chimney, the house is constantly filled with smoke . . .'

By the Fireside • *Charles Edward Wilson*

By the Fireside • *Charles Edward Wilson*

Even on a fine summer's day most cottages at the end of the last century were dark and dismal inside. Small windows, often with opaque glass, and an open door were the only sources of light. Today with electricity it is difficult to imagine how dark they must have been.

In the evening, the poorer cottagers used to rely on the red-glow of the fire or on rushlights for illumination. Rushlights were made from peeled rushes which were then dipped in grease. Gertrude Jekyll in her book *Old West Surrey* (1904) describes how a cottager friend of hers made them: 'You peels away the rind from the peth, leaving only a little strip of rind. And when the rushes is dry you dips'em through the grease, keeping'em well under. And my mother she always laid hers to dry in a bit of hollow bark. Mutton fat's the best; it dries hardest.' It was then placed in a rushlight holder which held it at an angle by being gripped by two pincers (unlike candles, they do not burn if held vertically). Candles, which gave off a stronger light, were also used but only on special occasions as they were much more expensive. Thomas Hardy in his short story *The Three Strangers* (1883) gives a vivid description of a cottage interior at night: 'The room was lighted by half a dozen candles, having wicks only a trifle smaller than the grease which enveloped them, in candlesticks that were never used but at high-days, holy-days, and family feasts. The lights were scattered about the room, two of them standing on the chimney-piece . . . On the path, in front of a back-brand to give substance, blazed a fire of thorns, that crackled "like the laughter of the fool".' Candles were later superseded by the more convenient paraffin lamp. The picture on the left shows both a paraffin lamp and a candle, the new replacing the old.

Mother and Child • *Carlton Alfred Smith*

A Time for Rest • *Carlton Alfred Smith*

A Cottage Interior • *Carlton Alfred Smith*

The interior of a cottage would usually be a better indicator of the social position and wealth of the inhabitant than the exterior. The picture above suggests that it belonged to a poor farm labourer living on the standard wage of ten shillings a week. The walls are crumbling, the furniture is very basic and there is no hint of any luxury. The scene reminds one of the description of workmen's cottages in Flora Thompson's *Lark Rise*: 'In nearly all the cottages there was but one room downstairs, and many of these were poor and bare, with only a table and a few chairs and stools for furniture and a superannuated potatosack thrown down by way of hearthrug.'

The interior on the left, with its finely dressed girls, pictures, ornaments, rug and upholstered furniture indicates that this belongs to someone of a higher social status and to someone who can afford more than the basic necessities. A detailed description of the inside of a 'bourgeois' cottage is given by Anthony Trollope in *Rachel Ray* (1863): 'close upon the green . . . was the pretty cottage of Mrs. Ray . . . It was a pretty place, with one small sitting-room opening back upon the little garden, and with another somewhat larger fronting towards the road and the green . . . Many of the widow's neatest belongings were here preserved in most perfect order; . . . There were shells on the chimneypiece and two or three china figures. There was a birdcage hung in the window but without a bird. It was all very clean, but the room conveyed at first glance an overpowering idea of its own absolute inutility and vanity . . .'

A Farm near Crewkerne • *Helen Allingham*

It is easy to be under the impression that Victorian cottage gardens were a riot of hollyhocks, asters and delphiniums. In fact, the priority for most cottage gardeners was to help feed a large family or supplement their meagre incomes. The cultivation of 'old-fashioned' flowers took a secondary role to growing vegetables, in particular potatoes, as Flora Thompson describes in *Lark Rise*: 'The garden was reserved for green vegetables, currant and gooseberry bushes, and a few old-fashioned flowers. Proud as they were of their celery, peas and beans, cauliflowers and marrows . . . their potatoes were their special care for they had to grow enough to last the year round.' The picture above shows how cabbages were grown alongside flowers.

Part of the garden would be kept for growing herbs which were used either to flavour rather bland food or for medicinal reasons, and the roots and leaves were used for dyeing clothes. Flora Thompson recorded some of their uses: 'the women cultivated a herb corner, stocked with thyme and parsley and sage for cooking, rosemary to flavour the home-made lard, lavender to scent the best clothes, and peppermint, pennyroyal, horehound, camomile, tansy, balm, and rue for physic. They made a good deal of camomile tea, which they drank freely to ward off colds, to soothe the nerves, and as a general tonic . . . The horehound was used with honey in a preparation to be taken for sore throats and colds on the chest.'

Peeling Potatoes • *Myles Birket Foster*

Spring Blossom in a Garden at Elstow • *Lilian Stannard*

The primary concern of the cottage gardener was to grow fruit and vegetables to feed his family but after the middle of the nineteenth century the cultivation of flowers and plants was commonplace. Cottagers took tremendous pride in their gardens and in their planting skills for not only was it a pleasurable and inexpensive hobby but the flowers supplied a much needed screen of colour to offset the dun-coloured thatch and decaying walls of the cottage. The scent from the flowers was also a pleasant way to hide less sanitary odours.

The focus of most cottage gardens centred around the cottage path which led from the cottage door to the garden gate by the side of the road. Here, one would typically see hollyhocks, asters, pinks, stocks, sweet peas, pansies, sunflowers and delphiniums. The garden would also typically have plants in pots scattered around the walls of the cottage and often a basic framework was built to train clematis and climbing roses.

The attractions of the cottage garden were commented upon by a number of the leading garden writers of the day. William Robertson wrote in *The English Flower Garden* (1883) that 'English cottage gardens are never bare and seldom ugly. Those who look at sea or sky or wood see beauty that no art can show; but among the things made by man nothing is prettier than an English cottage garden, and they often teach lessons that "great" gardeners should learn' and Gertrude Jekyll wrote in *Wood and Garden* (1899): 'I have learnt much from the little cottage gardens that help to make our English waysides the prettiest in the temperate world. One can hardly go into the smallest cottage garden without learning or observing something new'. The cottage on the right belonged to the bellringer at Witley church and was used for meetings of the Sunday School and the Mother's Union. It still stands today.

A Garden in Spring • *Helen Allingham*

An Old Well, Brook, Surrey • *Helen Allingham*

When we visit a cottage we take running water for granted. In fact, piped water was not common in many cottages until after the First World War.

In the nineteenth century, a small amount of rain water would be collected in a water butt at the side of the cottage (this water was considered to be the best for a woman's complexion) but for the majority of the cottagers' needs it came from a well or a nearby brook. Usually, a well was shared but if one lived at some distance from other cottages then a long, arduous journey was necessary. Carrying water was backbreaking work and sometimes women and children would make many trips to the well each day. The water was necessary for cooking, cleaning and washing clothes. Normally, a wooden pail attached to a chain, as in the picture on the left, was lowered from a winch into a deep well. If the water in the well was quite close to the surface then a long wooden pole with an iron hook fixed to the end was used to lower the pail. To protect children from falling in, a hinged wooden covering was placed across the top after use. Some cottagers jealously guarded their water as Flora Thompson wrote in *Lark Rise*: 'In dry summers, when the hamlet wells failed, water had to be fetched from a pump at some farm buildings half a mile distant. Those who had wells in their gardens would not give away a spot, as they feared if they did theirs, too, would run dry, so they fastened down the lids with padlocks and disregarded all hints.'

Well-digging was a laborious process often done by stone-diggers which required many weeks digging before lining the hole with curved bricks. The biggest problem which was impossible to predict was encountering a layer of rock at some feet below the surface which explains the odd location of some wells.

Newchurch, Isle of Wight • *Helen Allingham*

East End Farm, Pinner • *Helen Allingham*

East End Farm, Pinner • *Helen Allingham*

This fourteenth-century cottage is probably the oldest in Pinner in Middlesex, dating back to the same time as Pinner Parish Church. It is an example of a building which was protected by the SPAB (the Society for Protection of Ancient Buildings formed by William Morris in 1877) meaning that it could not be demolished or altered in any way. The chimney in the centre of the roof is particularly unusual in that it starts on the first floor and is supported all the way up by projecting beams; the chimney on the right of the cottage still has its original Tudor brickwork. Helen Allingham painted a number of farmhouses in Pinner in the 1890s, often accompanied by her friend and fellow artist Kate Greenaway. She wrote about her trips into the countryside with Kate Greenaway: 'During the summer we continued our outdoor work together . . . She was always scrupulously thoughtful for the convenience and feelings of the owners of the farm or cottage we wished to paint, with the consequence that we were made welcome to sit in the garden or orchard where others were refused admittance.'

It is interesting to compare these two watercolours of the same cottage from different perspectives.

The Village • *T. Hampson Jones*

The White Horse, Shere, Surrey • *Helen Allingham*

For most of the nineteenth century, the village was the focal point of both rural life and labour – you were born and brought up there, worked and died there. Usually, the village consisted of labourers' cottages lining either side of the road, an inn, a few shops, the manor house and the church and rectory. Villages evolved naturally over many years and much of their character, unlike model villages, stems from their lack of a cohesive structure and as Thomas Hardy wrote, 'every village has its idiosyncracy, its constitution'. The picture above shows a typical country village scene with a traveller and his horse and cart resting outside an inn. This peaceful existence ended with the introduction of modern transport.

Before the widespread use of trains and motor vehicles, most villages were quite isolated and visited only rarely by people other than travelling traders; visitors were looked upon as 'furriners'. However, the rapid increase in the size of towns and cities towards the end of the century put pressure on surrounding villages and many of them were swallowed up to become part of modern suburbia. Those that retained their isolation soon came under pressure from tourists looking for their idea of rural charm.

By the Old Cottage • *Helen Allingham*

These two pictures show different interpretations of the cottage. One shows a multi-coloured garden, a picturesque tumbledown cottage and a precarious chimney silhouetted against a cerulean sky with children playing happily outside. Sadly, the reality of the scene would have been more like the dark and dismal cottage above with its crumbling walls, cramped and cold interior. The cottage offered little comfort as is shown in Tom Taylor's poem of 1863 which strips away the sentimentality from any preconceived notions of cottage life:

I know. . . , too, the plagues that prey
On those who dwell in these bepainted bowers:
The foul miasma of their crowded rooms,
Unaired, unlit, with green damps moulded o'er,
The fever that each autumn deals its dooms
From the rank ditch that stagnates by the door;
And then I wish the picturesqueness less,
And welcome the utilitarian hand
That from such foulness plucks its masquing dress,
And bids the well-aired, well-drained cottage stand,
All bare of weather-stain, right-angled true,
By sketchers shunned, but shunned by fevers too.

Perhaps the reason why many of the cottage artists continued to paint idyllic views of children and cottages is commercial. There was a huge public demand for the nostalgia evoked by 'bepainted bowers'.

A Country Cottage • *Henry John Sylvester Stannard*

Naughty Boy • *Sir Hubert von Herkomer*

CHAPTER TWO

A PORTRAIT OF COUNTRY LIVING

In E. M. Forster's *Howard's End* (1910), the formidable Mr Wilcox says rather irritably to Helen Schlegel: 'A word of advice. Don't take up that sentimental attitude over the poor . . . the poor are poor, and one's sorry for them, but there it is . . . There are just rich and poor, as there always have been and always will be. Point me out a time when men have been equal.' This declaration is more than one man's attitude to life but encapsulates the entrenched Victorian view that every man had his place in society and that he should not try to alter this. The pictures in this book are, to a large extent, visual parallels painted by people who came from different backgrounds to their subjects and had no wish to question the accepted social order. They captured a way of life but from an outsider's point of view rather than the cottagers', as A. L. Baldry wrote in *The Practice of Watercolour Painting* (1911) they 'disregard the grimmer aspects of life'.

The conflict is between the observer and the observed. The diarist the Reverend Francis Kilvert, who gives us a detailed account of Victorian country life in the 1870s, views rural life like the artists in this book, seeing only the dignity and virtuosity attained through living a simple life. He records 'How delightful it is in these sweet summer evenings to wander from cottage to cottage and from farm to farm exchanging bright words and looks with the beautiful girls at their garden gates and talking to the kindly people sitting at their cottage doors or meeting in the lane when their work is done'. He continues: 'over the thick waving fragrant grass came the sweet country music of the white-sleeved mowers whetting their scythes and the voices of play among the fresh-cut flowery swaths'. His romantic imagery is, however, at odds with Thomas Hardy's description of working in the fields in *Tess of the D'Urbervilles* (1891). 'They worked on hour after hour, unconscious of the forlorn aspect they bore in the landscape, not thinking of the justice or injustice of their lot . . . In the afternoon the rain came on again . . . the rain had no occasion to fall, but raced along horizontally upon the yelling wind, sticking into them like glass splinters till they were wet through.' These two glimpses of Victorian rural life could not be more different so what was rural life really like for the cottager and his family at the end of the nineteenth century?

There is no doubt that life was hard and difficult and that the greatest enemies the cottager struggled against were the weather, hunger and poverty. The only form of heating was from the fire and, as a result, this was the focal point of cottage life. The fire was also used for cooking and boiling water for washing. Food was always in short supply and the cottagers were to a great extent self-sufficient. The garden, which in most of these pictures is depicted as a riot of colourful old-fashioned flowers, was principally used for growing fruit and vegetables; cabbages, potatoes, turnips and berries were a fundamental part of the cottagers' diet. Meat was rarely eaten except in small quantities and a man's lunch in the fields often consisted of only bread and lard or a piece of cheese, but the main meal in the evening would include a small piece of meat.

Most meat came from the cottage pig which was a vital part of both the cottage economy and society. They were bought as piglets (in the 1880s a piglet cost between twelve shillings and a pound depending on how plump it was), and fattened up until large enough to be slaughtered and kept in a pigsty at the side of the cottage, where they were fed on old refuse from the kitchen. It was always of great interest to neighbours to come and see the pig and, as Flora Thompson in *Lark Rise* says, the men-callers on a Sunday afternoon would come not to see the family but to scratch the pig's back and see how it was fattening up! When at last it was ready to be slaughtered the pig-sticker was summoned and the pig killed. The timing was important for it was believed that the bacon would shrink if the pig was killed outside the first two quarters of the moon. The killing was one of the most grisly images of cottage life as the pig was hoisted high by its legs and its throat

Will you have a taste? • *Carlton Alfred Smith*

carefully cut letting the blood flow freely; it was important not to let the pig die before the blood was fully drained or the meat would be ruined. In Thomas Hardy's *Jude the Obscure* (1895) the ritual is recorded like a macabre murder and the dilemma Jude faces is between the need to survive and the morality of it:

'Thank God!' Jude said. 'He's dead.'

'What's God got to do with such a messy job as pig-killing, I should like to know!' she said scornfully.

'Poor folks must live.'

After the pig was dead every part of it was used, for instance, the pig's head was made into brawn, the intestines into faggots and the blood into black pudding. Despite the importance of the pig it is rarely depicted by cottage artists probably for the practical reason that its image was not acceptable to the buying public.

The essence of cottage life and its culture can be found in such simple activities as breeding pigs, growing vegetables or beekeeping, all of which originated from economic necessity. Inextricably linked to these pursuits were superstitions which had evolved over centuries such as that recorded by Thomas Hardy in his short story *Interlopers at the Knap* (1884): 'It was the universal custom thereabout to wake the bees by tapping at their hives whenever a death occurred in the household, under the belief that if this were not done the bees themselves would pine away and perish during the ensuing year.' Superstitions varied from area to area but always related to the confines of their rural experiences. With the opening up of the urbane world to even the most remote and isolated parts of the country, the meaning and importance of such superstitions evaporated.

For cottagers who had no other transport than a horse and cart, travel was restricted to their own area and so even a journey of only a few miles to another village was considered quite an excursion. As a result, each community had its own identity, customs and crafts. Information was passed by word of mouth rather than in books and as life changed with the impact of the Industrial Revolution, so people like Gertrude Jekyll, the influential gardener and writer, were eager to record how people lived in Surrey before 'country folk' were swallowed up by the encroaching borders of London. Traditional crafts and materials which had barely changed over the centuries were being superseded by cheap imports and by the time many of these pictures were painted life had already changed dramatically. The peace of the countryside by the 1870s was now disrupted by the noise of the steam threshing machine.

Afternoon Tea • *Myles Birket Foster*

Poverty was a fact of life for cottagers, something one learnt to live with rather than fight against, and a well-known expression at the time was 'Poverty's no disgrace, but 'tis a great inconvenience'. The standard weekly wage for a man working in the fields was little more than ten shillings a week which only increased at certain times of the year, such as at harvest time. However, if the man did a more skilled job such as mending fences or thatching then he was paid an extra few shillings. It was not until the 1890s that a labourer's wage was increased to fifteen shillings a week. Even this higher wage was hardly adequate to bring up a large family (often families had as many as ten children) which is why most mothers worked either in the fields with their husbands or at home making straw baskets or lace. Women often rose before five to start their work and would not finish until the evening when they would then start their household chores. Children were also considered a vital part of the economic structure and were called upon to help either at home or work on the land. Often, this involved travelling great distances and working long hours for which they were paid a pittance. The introduction of the Education Act in 1870 and the Agricultural Children's Act of 1875 made little difference for a number of years. Contemporary records show that school took second place to helping on the land and parents were often reluctant to allow children to attend school, especially during the summer when they were needed most. The majority of children did not stay at school beyond the age of eleven.

Judging from the delightful pictures in this book children, who set the emotional and sentimental tenor, lived in a totally carefree world and are very rarely shown doing anything other than enjoying the sunshine by the cottage gate. Perhaps the explanation for this is that the cottage artists must have seen them as the innocent victims of the changes taking place at the end of the nineteenth century. The artists cannot have been unaware of the miserable lives which some of them lived, it was more a matter of ignoring this aspect and using artistic licence to achieve their own ends. The illusion of paradise is firmly contradicted by W. Cooke Taylor who wrote in *Factories and the Factory* (1844): 'We have seen children perishing from sheer hunger in the mud-hovel, or in the ditch by the wayside, where a few sods and withered boughs had formed a hut, compared with which a wigwam were a palace . . . There are no tasks imposed on young persons in factories that are anything near so laborious as hand-weeding corn, haymaking, stone-picking, potato-picking.'

The degree of poverty was also determined by which part of the country the cottage dweller lived in. Although these pictures are based on an idealized perception of rural life one can see that the cottagers appear to be better off in the south than those living in the remoter parts of Wales or Scotland. Here, even Myles Birket Foster paints them wearing rags and living in falling down hovels exposed to the full force of the elements. However, being poor did not necessarily mean a miserable and demeaning life as Flora Thompson, who grew up in a small hamlet in Oxfordshire in the 1880s, records in her autobiographical book *Lark Rise*: 'But, in spite of their poverty and the worry and anxiety attending it, they were not unhappy, and, though poor, there was nothing sordid about their lives.'

The greatest threat to rural life came not from isolation but from progress and the spread of suburbia. With the changes brought about by the machine age everywhere suddenly became accessible. Trains made travel quick and relatively easy and so travelling large distances was seen in terms of hours rather than days. The consequence of this was that a country way of life which had remained the same for centuries altered rapidly. Large cities were now easy to reach and the higher wages lured many away from the countryside and soon only a third of the people living in cities and large towns were actually born there. The ease of travel broke down the barriers between urban sophistication and rural simplicity. Cottage life and its indigenous culture virtually disappeared overnight and the traditional way of working the land was superseded by machines which required less manpower. Rural life by the first decade of this century had changed forever. The issue for many was not just the rapidity with which change was taking place but the fact that there was no record of what was being lost. This concerned Thomas Hardy who, in a letter written to Rider Haggard in 1902, wrote: 'For one thing village tradition – a vast mass of unwritten folk-lore, local chronicle, local topography, and nomenclature – is absolutely sinking, has nearly sunk, into eternal oblivion.'

Outside the Cottage • *Myles Birket Foster*

'Poverty's no disgrace but 'tis a great inconvenience' was a familiar saying among cottage people and behind this lay a tacit acceptance of their lot and a dignified acknowledgement that it was unlikely to change. Most cottagers earned their living by working on the land and by the end of the nineteenth century the weekly wage for a farm labourer of ten shillings had changed little from a hundred years before. This money was only just adequate to pay for their most basic needs such as food and clothing and with the lure of higher wages in the large cities it is not altogether surprising that the number of farmworkers fell from 1,483,000 in 1851 to little more than 650,000 by the first decade of this century.

Families were usually large, sometimes with as many as ten children, which increased the economic pressures to such an extent that it proved a great hardship to keep children at home beyond the age of ten or eleven. The cottages were often only built large enough for two people to live in which resulted in overcrowding and insanitary conditions. The man's paltry income meant it was essential to supplement this by growing his own fruit and vegetables and, if he could afford it, by keeping a pig or chickens. Although women would often help by selling lace or straw baskets which they had made, they sometimes also worked in the fields digging or hoeing, accompanied by their children if necessary, and for six hours' work a day they would be paid about four shillings a week.

While most of the pictures in this book concentrate on an idealized view of cottage life, both of these pictures show the harsh reality of life for many cottagers. Flora Thompson in *Lark Rise* observed that there was no room for luxuries in the 1880s: 'Coal at a shilling a hundred weight and a pint of paraffin for lighting *had* to be squeezed out of the weekly wage; for boots, clothes, illness, holidays, amusements, and household renewals there was no provision whatsoever.'

Irish Cottages • *Helen Allingham*

Buy a Broom • *Myles Birket Foster*

One of the most familiar sights on the village roads and country lanes was the wandering traders. There was a large demand for them and many would travel many miles a day, usually on foot, between hamlets and villages to sell their wares.

Most travellers, like the one selling brooms in the picture on the left, would acquire their materials from a local copse or forest. The wood found there could be used for making chairs, hoops, brooms or hurdles, all things which were easily transportable. In the autumn faggots, which were sticks or twigs cut or found loose in the undergrowth, were bundled up and sold at one and sixpence a score.

Other travellers would sell exotic fruit like tomatoes, which were a novelty at this time as they had only recently been introduced to England, and other unusual items like oranges. Tinkers used to arrive with their pots and pans and often they would bring grindstones to sharpen knives. Their arrival at a hamlet was often heralded by a song:

Any razors or scissors to grind?
Or anything else in the tinker's line?
Any old pots or kettles to mend?

Gipsy women would sell lavender, clothes pegs or cheap crockery, but if these were not required they would simply tell your fortune. Cheap jacks, packmen, egglers and tallymen were frequent visitors to the roadside cottages but by the turn of the century most had disappeared.

Those who had no items to sell sold their labour, especially at harvest time when large numbers of people (many came from Ireland) roamed the countryside offering their services. Others scraped a living by entertaining the children with animals like monkeys or by playing musical instruments, or by mending chairs as in the picture on the right.

The Chair Mender • *Myles Birket Foster*

Home Lessons • *Charles Edward Wilson*

Looking at the watercolour on the right of children returning from school, we are given the impression that education was a natural part of a child's upbringing. The reality was, in fact, rather different. Sending children to the local school was considered by most parents living in poor rural areas a nuisance at best and a waste of potential income at worst. Children were counted upon to make an important contribution to the economy of cottage life. The boys were expected to work in the fields doing jobs such as hop-picking, apple-picking or bird scaring and the girls to make lace or straw baskets.

During the 1860s, there was general concern about the lack of attendance at schools in rural districts and about the long hours worked by young children on the land. This resulted in several commissions being set up which culminated in the Agricultural Children's Act of 1875 which effectively stopped children under the age of ten from doing farm work. This increased the numbers of children going to school but it was many years before full attendance was achieved.

At school, the emphasis was on learning the basics such as reading and writing but arithmetic and Scripture were also considered important. The school itself was often a makeshift building with no lavatories, heating or water and some children had to walk many miles each day to get there.

The picture on the left shows a young boy who has returned from school and is writing on a slate with his leather satchel by his chair. The smock he is wearing was by this date out of fashion and in his reminiscences the artist Charles Edward Wilson recalls sketching outside a school in Shere in Surrey and seeing a young boy being bullied and teased for being the last person there to wear the smock which had been superseded by corduroy breeches.

Out of School • *Myles Birket Foster*

Playing Marbles • *Charles Edward Wilson*

The picture on the right shows two young girls playing cat's cradle outside a cottage. Of course, in the late nineteenth century the children of a farm labourer would not have had the sophisticated toys of today's generation, but would occupy themselves by making use of the simplest materials such as, in this case, a piece of string. Girls were also often seen playing with skipping ropes which were made from old discarded pieces of rope like that used for washing lines.

After a certain age, boys no longer played games with girls but instead went fishing or shooting birds with their catapults or playing football with an old blown up pig's bladder. In the picture above the boys are playing marbles, which was the most popular game at this time. The marbles were made of glass with different coloured threads running through the middle and were called 'alleys'. Marbles were highly prized as they were expensive for the boys to buy at twenty a penny.

Cat's Cradle • *Caroline Paterson*

The Magpie • *Charles Edward Wilson*

For most cottagers their income was too small to allow much money to be spent on food so much of it was grown in their gardens or allotments. Their diet on the whole was quite nutritious but lacking in variety. Vegetables and fruit such as potatoes, cabbages, turnips, marrows, gooseberries and rhubarb formed the greater part of their diet. Meat was a luxury and only a small amount was eaten at any one time unless the 'family' pig had recently been slaughtered. For breakfast, the men ate large chunks of bread thickly coated with lard which was often flavoured with rosemary leaves. They took their lunch with them to the fields to eat at midday. This usually consisted of bread and cheese and, if one was lucky, a small cube of cold bacon which would be carefully sliced into a cottage loaf while beer, cider or cold tea from large earthenware bottles was drunk in copious quantities. The main meal of the day, 'tea', was eaten in the evening. Flora Thompson in *Lark Rise* describes this ritual: 'About four o'clock, smoke would go up from the chimneys as the fire was made up and the big iron boiler, or the three legged pot, was slung on the hook of the chimney-chain. Everything was cooked in the one utensil; the square of bacon, amounting to little more than a taste each; cabbage, or other green vegetables in one net, potatoes in another, and the roly poly swathed in a cloth . . . the vegetables would then be turned out into big round yellow crockery dishes and the bacon cut into dice, with much the largest cube upon Feyther's plate, and the whole family would sit down to the chief meal of the day.'

Afternoon Tea • *William Kay Blacklock*

Beehives • *Helen Allingham*

A familiar sight in cottagers' gardens was beehives. These were traditionally made from straw, as shown here, which was then bound together with hazel or withy and was bought from a passing pedlar or gypsy, or alternatively the cottagers often made their own. Later on, straw beehives or skeps were made of wood chiefly because they were easier to use but they had the disadvantage of being heavier to carry to a swarm. The honey was important to cottagers not only because they could eat it but also because it could be used as a sweetener (sugar was too expensive) and for beeswax and its sale often supplemented their small incomes.

One of the most delightful and amusing descriptions of beekeeping can be found in Flora Thompson's autobiographical *Lark Rise*: 'Every fine day, throughout the summer, she sat there "watching the bees". She was combining duty and pleasure, for, if they swarmed, she was making sure of not losing the swarm . . . When at last, the long-looked-for swarm rose into the air, Queenie would seize her coal shovel and iron spoon and follow it over cabbage beds and down pea-stick alleys, her own or, if necessary, other peoples', tanging the spoon on the shovel: Tang tang-tangety tang! She said it was the law that, if they were not tanged, and they settled beyond her own garden bounds, she would have no further claim to them. Where they settled, they belonged . . . So she would follow and leave her shovel to mark her claim, then go back home for the straw skep . . .'

Another well-known custom was that of telling bees if there had been a death in the cottage, the worry being that if one did not then the bees would die as well!

Both of these pictures show the same cottage which still stands today at Sandhills in Surrey and remains virtually unchanged since it was painted.

Spring Blossom • *Helen Allingham*

Gathering Flowers • *Myles Birket Foster*

First of May Garland Day • *Myles Birket Foster*

For children, one of the most important and exciting days of the year was the First of May, May Day. The end of winter was marked by festivities which included May games, the maypole and May dances, but towards the end of the last century all that remained of these ceremonies was the May Garland. In the picture above, we can see the frame around which flowers were carefully entwined to form the garland which was then hoisted high on wooden poles. In a village or hamlet a pretty girl would be chosen as the May Queen and she wore a crown of interwoven daisies. Gathering flowers, as in the picture on the left, was considered an important part of the festivities. The children would then walk in procession to various houses and sing May songs in the hope of receiving a few pennies which would be eagerly shared at the end of the day.

John Ruskin, who was a great promulgator of the traditional rustic way of life, was worried about the decline of interest in May Day ceremonies; he introduced to Whitelands Training College for Women Teachers in Chelsea a May Day Festival and soon the college was annually bedecked with wild flowers from the countryside. As interest increased in old customs such as this, there was a notable resurgence of May Day festivities throughout the country in the 1880s and 1890s.

Washing Day • *Helen Allingham*

In the Spring • *Helen Allingham*

One of the most time-consuming jobs in the cottage was washing. Often the mother started as early as four in the morning and would not finish until the following evening. If there was no rain water in the water butt, she would have to make long journeys to the well or brook which could be as much as half a mile away. She would return with the buckets suspended from a yoke across her shoulders and start the laborious job of hand washing each garment in a red-ware washing pan as in the picture on the left. When the washing-pan broke an alternative use for it was found covering beehives.

Many women supplemented their husbands' income by doing laundry work for people living in 'the large houses', and a familiar sight in cottage gardens was long washing-lines of billowing clothes which were then ironed with a simple smoothing iron heated on the hearth.

The cottage above, which still stands near Hambledon in Surrey, was frequently painted by Helen Allingham. Today it looks very much as it did a hundred years ago, except for the kitchen chimney on the right which has been pulled down and the small upper window which has been blocked in.

Baking Bread • *Helen Allingham*

The picture on the right shows a young boy and his grandmother filling a cider barrel to take to his parents who would be working in the fields. The barrel, which was also called the harvest barrel, was made from oak and hooped with iron and made in varying sizes, the largest being able to hold as much as a gallon. To drink, the small cork was taken out of the wooden block and the barrel held aloft. In the picture, one can see how a leather cord was passed through the block which would be used as a carrying handle. The owner would also have his initials branded on at either end.

The cider was made by the cottagers themselves. After picking the apples, they were put into a cider mill which would pulp them into small pieces. The pulp was then put into fibre bags which were loaded between boards on a cider press and the juices forced out into a large barrel beneath. The simplicity of the process made it a good and cheap alternative to ale.

The charming watercolour on the left is one of the few examples of an interior scene by Helen Allingham. The pretty young woman is holding an oven peel which was used to place the dough in the oven. The oven was quite large and lined with brick. A fire was lit at the bottom of the oven and the heavy iron door was closed until the bricks had been heated to the correct temperature. Then the ashes were swept out and anything that needed baking like bread, cakes or puddings was placed inside; it was not uncommon to find little pieces of charcoal embedded on the underside of one's bread.

It is interesting that on the shelf above the mantle ruffle there are carefully depicted objects such as silver candlesticks, china figures, portrait miniatures and a rather anachronistic clock, details which suggest that this cottage belonged to someone other than a poor labourer.

The Cider Barrel • *Charles Edward Wilson*

An Afternoon in the Garden • *Myles Birket Foster*

Feeding Time • *Charles Edward Wilson*

The watercolour on the left shows young children helping in the cottage garden by planting flowers while the mother sits in the doorway looking after the smallest child. Gardening for children had been recommended by theorists since the middle part of the nineteenth century, not only because it was healthy to be working outside but also because the Victorians considered it was important that a work ethic was acquired at an early age.

A number of books on gardening were written for children such as Jane Louden's *My Own Garden: or the Young Gardener's Year Book* (1855), which was certainly influential among wealthier households. However, in a labourer's cottage gardening was a necessity rather than a pastime which is why in the picture on the left the cabbage in the foreground is given such prominence. In the picture above, the boy is trimming turnips which would have been grown in the cottage garden.

Harvest Time • *Myles Birket Foster*

Harvesting was the most important period in the farmers' calendar and large numbers of people were involved from the regular farmworker to his wife and children and casual labourers. The basic tools used for harvesting were the same that had been used for centuries, that is, the fagging hook, the scythe, the sickle and the reaping hook. These continued to be used until machinery, like the early mowing machine, was introduced in the 1890s, but it was some time before harvesting became totally mechanized.

The men would cut the corn by holding it up with a stick and then cutting across with a fagging hook or scythe. After this, the loose corn or wheat was tied together forming sheaves which were then made into shocks. A shock usually consisted of twelve corn sheaves stood on end with their heads resting together; it was only barley which could be left on the ground overnight as it was not spoilt by the weather. Afterwards, the corn was stacked in large barns where it was threshed and winnowed before being stored in granaries.

During harvest time, work would start at first daylight and the first break would be at six for breakfast. Lunch was between nine and ten, dinner at midday, afternoon lunch at four and supper at seven. Most of these meals would vary little from bread eaten with lard, cheese, or if available a piece of meat. The harvesters would also take with them iron-hooped barrels or earthenware jugs of beer or cider which was drunk from as often as possible and it was not uncommon for fights to break out in the fields after the workers had had too much ale in the midday sun. Some farmers would supply food for their workers and it was usual for them to mark the end of the harvest with a harvest home supper which was one of the biggest celebrations of the year.

Harvest Time near Holmbury Hill, Surrey • *George Vicat Cole*

The Gleaners • *Myles Birket Foster*

Return from Gleaning • *James Fahay*

Gleaning or leazing occurred at the end of the harvest when women and children collected fallen grain from between the stubble. In the picture above the gleaners are returning home in the evening after being fortunate enough to collect whole sheaves as well as individual ears. The gleanings were an important part of cottage life as they could keep a family in flour for many months and the straw would be used for making either baskets or mending chairs.

Gleaning was a common right but throughout the nineteenth century farmers tried to curb the practice, especially where certain crops were concerned. But many farmers were happy to allow their own workers to glean crops, like wheat, not only because it was considered part of the working contract but also because it cleared the ground for winter ploughing.

It was, however, backbreaking work as Flora Thompson illustrates in *Lark Rise*: 'Up and down and over and over the stubble they hurried, backs bent, eyes on the ground, one hand outstretched to pick up the ears, the other resting on the small of the back . . . It was hard work, from as soon as possible after daybreak until nightfall . . . but the single ears mounted, and a woman with four or five strong, well-disciplined children would carry a good load home on her head every night.'

The Necklace • *Carlton Alfred Smith*

One of the favourite pastimes of children was to rob a nest of its eggs. The eggs were then blown (the child would often eat the raw contents) and made into a necklace with a string passed through it, like the one the girl is holding in the picture above, or simply put on display on a shelf at home. Country custom meant that certain birds' nests, like that of a wren, robin or swallow, were not allowed to be interfered with.

Songbirds were considered a delicacy and boys used to spend hours hunting them in the hedgerows with their catapults. If nets were used as many as ten could be caught at one time and the birds, which were usually sparrows, chaffinches or thrushes, were either made into a large pastry pie or roasted on a stick in front of a fire. Bird traps were also a common sight in cottage gardens which worked by attaching a piece of string to a balanced wooden box which was then pulled on to the bird.

Some men made a living out of catching songbirds alive and sending them to London to be sold in the markets. It was also very common to keep birds like magpies in a wicker cage.

Poaching was also widely practised and could form an important additional source of income or meal for the cottager's family. However, if a man was caught stealing a pheasant from a farmer's land then the penalty was very severe.

The Bird's Nest • *Charles Edward Wilson*

Blackberry Time • *Myles Birket Foster*

Fruit picking in counties such as Kent and Somerset provided the cottage family with an important additional source of income. It was usually done by women and children as the men would be working in the fields but after the harvest, when jobs were more difficult to find, men would help pick apples which were the last of the fruits to be gathered. Apples would be sent up to the markets in London, sold locally, or made into cider.

Children were much in demand for picking raspberries, strawberries, gooseberries and currants as their smaller fingers were considered less likely to damage the crops! Contemporary records show that there was a high level of absenteeism from school when a local farmer or landowner needed fruit picking.

In the picture on the left, children are looking in the hedgerows for blackberries and elderberries, both of which were used for making pies or for home-made wine. Jam, a great luxury for children, was also made from hedgerow fruit, as was crabapple jelly.

Labourers were also actively encouraged to grow fruit in their own garden, however small it was. Dean Hole wrote, rather patronizingly in *Our Gardens* (1902) that the cottager 'should have apple-tree, plum tree and cherry tree, his bushes of gooseberries and currants . . . in addition to his gardens of flowers', ignoring the fact that most cottage gardens were first and foremost used to grow foodstuffs.

Picking Fruit • *Carlton Alfred Smith*

Carrying Hay • *Helen Allingham*

Most cottagers were farm labourers which involved rising early and being in the fields soon after daybreak. The work was hard and monotonous and continued heedless of the weather. They were considered the backbone of the agricultural world who could plough, dig ditches, mow, pull potatoes or help with the various harvests. For this, they were paid ten shillings a week and harvest time was the only opportunity they had to supplement this. Skilled labourers like sheep shearers or blacksmiths earned an extra two shillings a week. Regular work was always a problem for agricultural workers as Rider Haggard in *Rural England* (1906) explained: 'Of course the lowness of the wage and the lack of prospect will always cause a great number . . . to desert the land, but I am convinced that there are large numbers who would bide in their villages if only they could be sure of constant work.'

The carter, seen in the picture on the right, would have to get up earlier than other labourers in order to feed and prepare his horses for the day's work. He was always very proud of his horses and dressed them up with engraved brass plates, rosettes and brightly coloured ear caps.

As machinery played a more and more important role in farming life so the traditional hierarchy of agricultural society changed. Less labourers were needed and consequently more men left the fields to work in the factories of the big towns and cities. By the first decade of the twentieth century, England's economy had changed from one based on agriculture to one based on industry.

The Cart Horse • *Helen Allingham*

Raking Hay • *Helen Allingham*

The two pictures illustrated here show the different roles a rural woman had to combine, that of wage earner and mother. A woman's ability to earn money was an essential part of the cottage economy and she had to couple this with bringing up a family and doing the household chores such as cooking and washing. During the day, she would take her children into the fields with her or, if this was not possible, one of her elder children would stay at home and look after the younger ones.

On the land, a woman was expected to be strong and hard working, often doing the same physical work as men. Looking after cattle, stone-picking or helping with the harvest of wheat, corn, apples or hops were among the most common jobs. One of the least rewarding winter tasks was swede trimming. A vivid description of this is given in Thomas Hardy's *Tess of the D'Urbervilles* (1891): 'At this occupation they could shelter themselves by a thatched hurdle if it rained; but if it was frosty even their thick gloves could not prevent the frozen masses they handled from biting their fingers.' Turnip picking and potato pulling were also among the backbreaking jobs expected of them.

On a higher social scale than the woman field labourer was the dairymaid as her work was considered a skilled job. This required an ability to skim milk and make butter and cheese. The hours were long, lasting from daybreak until dusk.

It is interesting to observe that many of the Victorian artists who depicted women chose to paint an idyllic view of their life choosing to ignore the realities which the social-realist artists were at pains to show.

The Young Drover • *Myles Birket Foster*

The Cottage Gate • *Helen Allingham*

Children Playing • *Myles Birket Foster*

Both of these pictures suggest that children lived in a Utopian cocoon, a carefree world without any hardship. To a great extent, the impression we are given is false, based on artistic licence rather than truth. This was commented on by a critic in the Art Journal of 1888 in relation to Helen Allingham's work: 'there is no trace of sympathy with the stern realism to which we have grown accustomed . . . For her there would be little attractions of a pictorial kind in the marks of grime and toil on rugged hands and bronzed faces . . . Still less is it Mrs Allingham's province to portray the sadder phases of child-life . . .'

Most rural families were large, sometimes with as many as ten children living in cramped and often bitterly cold conditions.[1] Clothes were often inadequate and threadbare and the food monotonous and scarce. From a very early age, children were expected to help in and around the cottage collecting firewood, going to the well or helping to look after the younger children. Even after the Education Act was introduced in 1870, children would not attend school if they were needed to help with the hop-picking or the harvest. In 1867 a mother giving evidence to the Children's Employment Commission said that her two daughters, one aged eleven and the other fourteen, walked eight miles to work and eight miles back and after working for ten hours were paid seven shillings each.

A Stitch in Time • *Carlton Alfred Smith*

The style of rural clothing was determined by practical considerations and changed little over the centuries. Clothes were expected to last and a man's 'Sunday suit' would see him through to the end of his life. Until the middle of the nineteenth century, most labourers wore the traditional shapeless frock smock made of strong linen and a black felt hat. By the end of the century, most men wore suits of corduroy.

The old woman in the picture on the right is wearing a bonnet which would have been tied under her chin by a ribbon. On Sundays, she would put on her much cherished Sunday bonnet made of patterned black satin. Usually, a woman would wear just a muslin cap inside the cottage. Over her shoulders she wears a woollen shawl which in the summer would have been replaced by one made of cotton.

The young woman in the picture on the left wears a typical print gown and apron. Children's clothes were handed down from generation to generation depending on how poor the family was, which is why some boys still wore the old-fashioned smock long after it had gone out of fashion. The boy in this picture is wearing breeches and a waistcoat while the girl in the background wears a traditional cotton frock with a long pinafore. For the mother, clothing large families was always a problem. One of the most important sources of clothes came from families who had a daughter in service who would send back her employers' cast-offs.

Perhaps the most prized article of clothing was a good pair of boots. For most families, leather boots were a luxury but a very necessary item. The men wore hobnailed boots which were essential for working the fields while boys and girls wore heavy leather ones. When going over muddy or wet ground pattens were worn which were made of wood and raised several inches above the ground by iron hoops.

Forty Winks • *Charles Edward Wilson*

A Faithful Friend • *Carlton Alfred Smith*

Animals, usually accompanied by children, are one of the most unashamedly sentimental and nostalgic images of Victorian painting. The artist often chose to show a child looking after or feeding animals, like chickens as in the picture on the right, or holding a cat at the cottage gate, because it provided a focal point and because animals, like children, gave the impression of a natural and ideal world, a world of innocence lost to us by the Industrial Revolution.

Most animals are portrayed as pets even though the principal reason for cottagers keeping them was purely practical; the cat caught mice, the hens supplied eggs and the pig provided the meat which was one of the economic pillars of the cottage economy. Piglets were bought for between twelve and eighteen shillings each and fattened up until slaughtered. They were kept in a pigsty at the side of the cottage and fed on old refuse from the kitchen. When the pig was ready, the pig-sticker was summoned and a large feast followed the slaughter. Every part of the pig was used, the head being made into brawn, the intestines into faggots and the blood into black pudding.

If a cottager was wealthy enough he would also own a cow and the milk, which was considered a great luxury, would be sold by the jug to his neighbours.

The dog portrayed in the picture on the left must have belonged to the artist, Carlton Alfred Smith, as it appears in a number of works by him. The female model is also a favourite of his and she appears in the watercolour A Stitch in Time on the previous page. Charles Edward Wilson, who painted the picture on the right, often used the same models as Smith. Before moving to Surrey, they both shared the same studio in London.

Feeding the Chicks • *Charles Edward Wilson*

Plaiting Rushes • *Carlton Alfred Smith*

In the second half of the last century, traditional crafts which had been practised by women and children in their cottages for centuries began to disappear as the spread of industrialization meant machines could mass produce things hitherto made by hand. Straw and rush plaiting (as in the picture on the left), bead work, button-holing, making birch brooms, lace-making, and spinning were among the cottage crafts which were rapidly disappearing. The demise of these crafts was mourned by Gertrude Jekyll in her book *Old West Surrey* (1904): 'The sight of these simple pieces of mechanism [spinning wheels] makes one think how much fuller and more interesting was the rural home life of the older days . . . when people found their joy in life at home . . . surely that older life was better and happier and more fruitful.' Many of these crafts were related to particular areas so lace-making was widely practised in Devon and Bedfordshire, straw plaiting in Hertfordshire and Essex. Children were often sent to special schools in the village where they could learn these home industries and for their work they would be paid a small amount. Parents preferred their children to go to these schools rather than a normal school because their earnings were an important contribution to the cottage economy. The conditions they had to work in have been compared with those of a workshop with many children crammed into a small room in a cottage. The schools were run on a strict basis and the child was required to complete a certain amount of work each day. Ruskin and Morris were ardent advocates of the 'vital value' of cottage crafts. However, outside observers often failed to understand how these crafts were practised out of economic necessity rather than for personal enjoyment. Labour intensive cottage crafts soon became obsolete in the face of cheaper machine-made goods. It is interesting to note that the spinning wheel in the background of the picture on the right lies idle which provides an accurate comment on the changing times.

The Fairy Tale • *Carlton Alfred Smith*

Christmas Eve • *Carlton Alfred Smith*

The Watering Place • *Myles Birket Foster*

The church, through both its physical and spiritual presence, was the focal point of village life. It was also the only place which brought together all members of the village community, irrespective of class or wealth. There were, however, clear divisions regarding which pew one sat in depending on whether you were the squire, the farmer or the labourer, and the clergy in their sermons would often preach the observance of social categories as being a natural part of God's order.

On Sunday mornings, the church bells rang out loud summoning the congregation from the local village, nearby hamlets and isolated cottages. People came across the fields and over stiles from all different directions. At the end of the nineteenth century, the bells also performed the function of announcing the death of anyone in the village; a bell would be tolled three times for the death of a man, twice for the death of a woman and once for the death of a child.

Christmas was an important time for the cottagers because it meant that the men did not have to work on Christmas Day and it was an occasion to eat well as the farmer would contribute a joint of beef. The picture on the left shows a young woman who has just come in from the snow holding a large bundle of holly. Cottagers used to travel long distances to cut it, not only to decorate their houses with but also to sell for which they would be paid as much as half a crown for a large bundle.

Haymaking • *Edmund George Warren*

At the time these watercolours were painted the full impact of the effects of the Industrial Revolution were being felt by even the most remote rural areas. With the rapid growth of the railways, nowhere was more than a few hours from a major city. The result of this was that traditions and customs which had changed only gradually over the centuries were being threatened by the constant movement of the population.

Flora Thompson in *Lark Rise* laments how these changes threatened the structure of rural society: 'All times are times of transition; but the eighteen-eighties were so in a special sense, for the world was at the beginning of a new era, the era of machinery and scientific discovery. Values and conditions of life were changing everywhere. Even to simple country people the change was apparent. The railways had brought distant parts of the country nearer; machinery was superseding hand labour, even on the farms to some extent; . . . Horizons were widening; a stranger from a village five miles away was no longer looked upon as "a furriner".' Both of these pictures show a tranquil country scene with farm labourers working in a traditional way. The haycart pulled by horses and the raking of hay are evocative of this era which was soon to be replaced by the noisy steam threshing machine which went on hire from farm to farm.

Above the Farm • *Edmund George Warren*

Children Reading • *Myles Birket Foster*

CHAPTER THREE

THE WORLD OF THE COTTAGE ARTIST

The cottage artists enjoyed enormous popularity especially during the period 1870–1910. Undoubtedly, the most successful was Myles Birket Foster. E. M. Cundall, in his biography of the artist written in 1906, reached the conclusion that 'it may be asserted without fear of contradiction that the watercolour drawings executed by Birket Foster appeal to the British public more than the works of any other British artist'. Although this may be a somewhat partisan response there is no question that his pictures sold in large numbers and for high prices and one of them *The Arrival of Hop Pickers*, *Farnham* sold for five hundred pounds in 1890, a colossal sum at that time. He exhibited regularly at the Royal Academy and at the Royal Society of Painters in Watercolour and with established London fine art dealers such as L&W Vokins and Agnews. His wide popularity is all the more surprising when viewed against the background of change in artistic aims and fashion which had taken place thirty years earlier and looking at his work it is easy to forget that he was working at the same time as Whistler, Sickert and Steer. *The Times* after his death in 1899 wrote: 'It is remarkable that up to the very end, even in days when modern English art was passing through a period of great depression, and when many more powerful artists found their work quite unsaleable, Mr Birket Foster's drawings always sold.' Contemporary comments such as this illustrate how his safe, repetitive and conventional representations of the rural world fulfilled the expectations of what many Victorians wanted from a picture. There was a section of the buying public, as today, to whom the colour experiments of the continental artists were anathema and they wanted above all else pictures that did not challenge their preconceived ideas of art. In an obituary after Birket Foster's death a journalist summed up his success, and by doing so the success of the other cottage artists, by writing that his pictures were 'always conscientious and they were the sort of art that people could understand.' The demand for his work can be further gauged by the extraordinary lengths people went to in order to fake it. These range from poor copies of his prints to highly competent interpretations of his style and technique. Birket Foster was often asked to authenticate his own work and even registered his monogram as a trade mark.

The nostalgic desire to own a picture of the countryside is also reflected in Helen Allingham's commercial success. After the death of her husband in 1889, she brought up her family on the proceeds from the sale of her pictures of cottages. Commercial galleries in London like The Fine Art Society held exhibitions devoted to her pictures and many of these were bought by the professional classes, in particular by doctors and lawyers. Other people who are recorded as buying her pictures are the poet Alfred, Lord Tennyson, the Master of the Rolls and the President of the Glasgow Chamber of Commerce. Like Birket Foster, Allingham travelled abroad and painted views of cities such as Venice and Verona but she found these less easy to sell than her cottage pictures. Today, after a period of neglect her work is once again sought after and some of her pictures can sell for over forty thousand pounds at auction.

The commercial potential of views of rural life resulted in the publication of several books illustrated with the watercolours of Helen Allingham. The two most popular were *The Happy England of Helen Allingham* (1903) and *The Cottage Homes of England* (1909). The nostalgic titles are revealing in themselves reflecting both Allingham's and the general public's idyllic view of country life. The introduction of new colour reproduction techniques resulted in many of the illustrations being framed and sold.

Perhaps the perpetuation of an idealized view of life can in part be accounted for by the comfortable lives the artists lived compared with those of their subjects. Both Birket Foster and Allingham were born into quite wealthy middle-class families and although they worked hard to achieve their success lived comfortable lives.

When Birket Foster first moved to Witley in Surrey in 1860, he rented a cottage called Tigbourne Cottage which he used as a base while overseeing the building of his new house called The Hill which has been described as 'an essay in Victorian Tudorism' and was a large and imposing house with twenty acres of land. The interior was decorated by William Morris's company Morris, Marshall, Faulkner and Co., which had been established in 1861. The pseudo-Medieval impression was added to by the stained glass windows made from the designs of Pre-Raphaelite artists like Burne-Jones, Rossetti and Ford Madox Brown. The grandeur of the house, with its important library and collection of pictures, was far removed from the peasant lives and cottages which he depicted and the gentrifying of the Surrey countryside prompted William Morris to complain that it 'looks more than most countrysides as if it were kept for the pleasures of the rich, as indeed it is'. However, although it is true that his sentimental approach fantasized a way of life of which he was a distant observer much of his work can also be seen in terms of wishing to glorify something which he and many others considered superior to the grime and ugliness of urban life.

Helen Allingham also lived in a large house in Witley called Sandhills, which she moved to with her family in 1881. It was not like any of the cottages which she painted having been built only nine years earlier in 1872 and it was one of the largest houses in the area with its own full-time gardener. William Morris described it rather deprecatingly as 'highly uninteresting though not specially hideous, nor the get up inside of it very pleasant (though not very bad), as you might imagine'. It was from here that she used to paint the surrounding cottages.

For Allingham, it was more the cottage and the hedgerow which were most important rather than the figures, which are the central part of a Birket Foster composition. W. Graham Robertson in his memoirs *Time Was* (1931) particularly admired her ability to penetrate to the soul of the English countryside: 'Her lovely little transcripts of the Surrey lanes and woodlands . . . are delights to the eye and lasting memorials of the fast-vanishing beauty of our countryside. In a few more years they will seem visions of a lost Fairyland.' In a picture by Myles Birket Foster, the figures are involved in some sort of activity like gardening or cottage crafts whereas Allingham's tend to be there to give scale to the cottage. Apart from the necessity to earn a living by selling her pictures both Helen and her husband William were concerned by the amount of cottages which were being pulled down or badly altered, and many were painted as a means of preserving a visual record of them and to draw attention to their destruction. When the Allinghams moved back to London in 1888, they moved into a large house in Hampstead but Helen Allingham continued to travel to Kent, Surrey and Sussex to paint.

What were Allingham and Birket Foster like as people? There is little doubt that Allingham was a very strong character, perhaps a reflection on her Unitarian upbringing. Her husband died when she was forty-one leaving her little money and she had to bring up three children through the sale of her watercolours. W. Graham Robertson in his memoirs *Time Was* (1931) gives a good insight into the type of person she was, someone who was both caring and not afraid of hard work: 'What would have happened to William Allingham had he not married Helen Paterson (Allingham) it is impossible to imagine. She understood him thoroughly, cared for him deeply and made life smooth and happy for him; and to do all this for a poet would have provided most women with a fairly arduous career. But she also had her work as an artist and she painted day in and day out; in fact she hardly ever seemed otherwise occupied.' She was also a modest person expressing great surprise when someone approached her to write an article about her life. Birket Foster, who came from a Quaker family in the north of England, seems to have been an immensely popular man judging from the number of contemporary quotes which praised him as much as a man as a painter. His house The Hill in Witley where he lived with his wife and family became a great meeting place for his friends, especially from the artistic and literary circles in London. In 1906, M. H. Spielmann wrote in *The Daily Graphic*, 'He will always be remembered as a very charming personality, a very personal watercolourist, whose tenderness of vision and delicacy of touch tickle and delight the eye of the public of taste, while he himself by reason of his own sweet nature and kindly outlook on life, has entered into the heart of the picture-loving public, and will be cherished there as an artist, as he is cherished as a man in the memory of his friends.'

The advantage of working in watercolour was that only a sketch book and a box of paints were needed to paint *en plein air* rather than the paraphernalia of an oil painter. Most of Helen Allingham's work was done in front of her subject and she is remembered by the owner of one cottage she painted perched on a stool wearing a black cloak and amber beads with her sketch book balanced on her knees. W. Graham Robertson also wrote of her in his memoirs *Time Was* (1931): 'My memories of her wit and wisdom are chiefly in the

A Surrey Cottage • *Helen Allingham*

shape of detached sentences, jerked over her shoulder as she sat at the bottom of a damp ditch, knee-deep in nettles, or poised precariously on a pigsty wall, using her open umbrella as an easel.' Later, she would finish the watercolour in her studio often using models for the figures, which is why many of her favourite sitters, such as Rhoda Hardy who ran the local inn, the Dog and Pheasant, at Brook, can be recognized in a number of her watercolours. In Jan Reynolds's book on Birket Foster she quotes from some papers in the Glasson family (descendants of the artist) which record his working methods: 'B.F. was an extraordinarily rapid sketcher and a friend who constantly went out with him used to complain that while he was deciding what to pencil in, B.F. had not only settled to his subject and drawn it in, but had half finished the colouring. He was also when sketching insensible to cold or heat, so wrapped up was he in his drawing . . . A watercolour folding palette ready charged with all the needful colours, a brush or two and a sketch book as large as his coat pocket or possibly a piece of Chalon board in brown paper was all he took on many occasions. He borrowed chairs at the cottages he loved to draw. He occasionally carried a sketching bag and camp stool but never an umbrella.'

Towards the end of the nineteenth century, a second generation of cottage artists were inspired by the success and example of Myles Birket Foster and Helen Allingham and moved to or near Witley, which now had a large artistic community living there. The two most successful of these were Charles Edward Wilson and Carlton Alfred Smith, both of whom had shared the same studio in London. Wilson, who like Allingham came from Derbyshire, did not become a professional watercolour painter until he was forty-one when he moved to Mousehill on Milford Common in Surrey. He bought a large heather-thatched barn which he used as both his studio and home. Like Birket Foster, he concentrated on painting children or young women working or playing but created an entirely different effect by using carefully controlled colours. Many of his works are of cottage interiors but like the other Witley artists there is little attempt to show the reality of living in a cramped and overcrowded cottage. Like Wilson, Carlton Alfred Smith was a member of the Royal Institute of Painters in Watercolours, founded in 1881, where he was a regular exhibitor. He also specialized in figures in an interior and often they used the same models dressed in clothes from the previous generation. His ability to paint the effects of light falling across a room from a window or from the light of a fire makes him one of the most technically accomplished Victorian watercolourists.

Henry John Sylvester Stannard worked mainly in the countryside of Bedfordshire where he painted to an unvarying formula of overtly sentimental views of cottages often with young children outside playing with a cat. His colours are more garish and pronounced than his predecessors but he received much recognition during his lifetime and enjoyed royal patronage.

Arthur Claude Strachan also tends to be repetitive concentrating on the archetypal thatched cottage with children at the door. He uses strong colour and his attention to detail can be seen in his meticulous delineation of every flower in the cottage garden.

A third generation of cottage artists were represented by people like David Woodlock and Thomas Mackay, both of whom used the cottage and cottage life as their main motif, but for them experimenting with a wide range of colour and techniques was more important than the traditional representational approach of Birket Foster and Allingham. In this respect their work is firmly entrenched in the twentieth rather than the nineteenth century.

Past Work • *Helen Allingham*

Although Helen Allingham spent most of her adult life in the south of England, she was born in Swadlincote in Derbyshire and was brought up near Altrincham where her father was a doctor. Her childhood was a happy one and her early talent for drawing was encouraged by her family. She studied at the Birmingham School of Design and later in 1868 at the Royal Academy Schools in London. It was while she was here that she needed to earn money for her widowed mother and so began her career by doing line illustrations for books and magazines such as *Once a Week*, *The Cornhill Magazine* and *The Graphic*, where she was also a reporter.

It was through her work that she met her future husband the poet William Allingham who, today, is chiefly remembered for his poem 'The Fairies' with its opening line, 'Up the airy mountain, Down the rushy glen'. He was twenty-three years Helen's senior and a well-known figure amongst the artistic and literary luminaries of the day. Subsequently, she met such people as Carlyle, Tennyson and Burne-Jones who became close friends.

By 1881, Helen had two children, Gerald and Eva, and it was in this year that they moved to Sandhills in Surrey. A year later her favourite child Henry was born, but despite having three children to look after she continued to work as hard as ever, painting hundreds of cottages in the area. She exhibited widely in London where her work was immensely popular and in 1886 she held an exhibition at The Fine Art Society devoted entirely to her Surrey cottages, which prompted a journalist in *The Times* to describe her work as 'the very model of what an English water-colour should be'.

On account of her husband's ill-health, the Allinghams left Surrey in 1888 and settled in Hampstead. William Allingham died a year later and it was typical of Helen's robust character that she managed to support her family through sheer hard work.

At Penstreet • *Helen Allingham*

Sandhills • *Helen Allingham*

At Sandhills, Witley • *Helen Allingham*

Sandhills (named after the sandhills there) was the small hamlet outside Witley in Surrey where Helen Allingham and her family moved to a large cottage which was also rather confusingly called Sandhills. By the time they moved back to London on account of William Allingham's ill-health in 1888, the area around them had become popular with artists interested in the cottage genre such as Charles Edward Wilson and Carlton Alfred Smith and the man who moved into the Allinghams' house, W. Graham Robertson, also attracted many of the most famous theatrical personalities of the day such as Ellen Terry.

The picture on the left is a view of Sandhills which was built in 1872 for the artist John Malcolm Stewart, a close friend of Myles Birket Foster. After Stewart became ill, his trustees Edmund Evans and Charles Keene were approached by William Allingham in 1881 who bought the lease. The Allinghams stayed there until 1888 and Helen Allingham must have painted this on one of her painting trips to Surrey in 1910.

The cottage in the picture above was lived in by the Allinghams' gardener, a man called John Hardy. In front of the fence stands his daughter-in-law Ada who is holding her baby, Ernest. Today, the sandpit has grown over but the yew tree still stands.

Near Freshwater, Isle of Wight • *Helen Allingham*

One of the most well-known books illustrating Helen Allingham's work is called *The Cottage Homes of England*. The title for the book originated from a poem published in 1838 by Felicia Dorothea Hemans who, like Allingham, extolled both the beauty and the concept of the cottage:

The cottage homes of England!
By thousands on her plain,
They are smiling o'er the silvery brooks
And round the hamlet fanes.

This was later parodied by the magazine *Punch*:

The cottage homes of England
Alas! How strong they smell
There's fever in the cesspool
And sewage in the well.

The two verses neatly sum up the perceived idea of cottage life through the eyes of the painter and the reality for the observed cottager in his home.

The picture on the left shows the idealized view of a well-manicured cottage with a mother and child happily standing at the cottage gate on a sunny day while the one on the right shows in an unusually forthright manner what the reality was for most cottagers – a delapidated hovel.

A Highland Cottage • *Myles Birket Foster*

A Cottage at Pinner • *Helen Allingham*

Shepherd's Hill, Haslemere • *Helen Allingham*

Criticism is often levelled at artists such as Helen Allingham or Myles Birket Foster, claiming that their work is too frivolous and sentimental. It is not always understood that there was a more serious intention behind many of their representations of rural cottages and English country life. They were part of a growing movement concerned about the destruction of our vernacular heritage by the spread of urbanization and by the insensitive restoration of cottages by unsympathetic builders.

One of the most influential champions of this cause was John Ruskin, who as early as 1840 had argued against the poor restoration and bastardization of old buildings: 'Do not let us talk . . . of restoration the thing is a lie from beginning to end.' His concerns motivated like-minded people and in 1877 William Morris created The Society for Protection of Ancient Buildings, an idea which probably originated from Ruskin's *Opening of the Crystal Palace* (1854) which called for the preservation of old buildings.

The seriousness of the situation was nicely summarized by William Allingham in his preface to the catalogue of one of Helen's exhibitions when he lamented that, 'in the short time, to be counted by months, since these drawings were made, no few (*sic*) of the Surrey Cottages, which they represent have been thoroughly "done up" and some of them swept away'.

The picture on the left is of a cottage in Pinner in Middlesex which both Kate Greenaway and Helen Allingham painted a few hours before it was demolished. The picture above shows cottages on Shepherd's Hill in Haslemere, Surrey. These were knocked down in the 1930s.

A Cottage at Farringford • *Helen Allingham*

Helen Allingham met Alfred, Lord Tennyson, the Poet Laureate, through her husband William after they were married in 1874. Tennyson and the Allinghams became great friends and after William's death in 1889, Helen was invited to Tennyson's large home on the Isle of Wight on a regular basis; while she was there she painted many of the surrounding cottages. Hallam, Tennyson's son, who was also a great friend, suggested she collaborate on a book with her brother Arthur Paterson called *Homes of Tennyson* which was published in 1905 with twenty illustrations of Allingham's work, one of which is reproduced on the left.

As a summer retreat Tennyson, who felt that the Isle of Wight was becoming too full of Cockneys, had a house built called Aldworth on Blackdown which was six miles from the Allinghams at Sandhills. He shared Allingham's deep concern about the preservation of cottages in the area and he used to point out ones she should paint. The picture on the right is of a cottage near Blackdown and was also reproduced in Paterson's *Homes of Tennyson*. In the text Helen wrote, 'One day when my husband and I were over from Witley Tennyson took us for a beautiful walk, within sight of this beautiful old cottage, but it was too muddy that day for us to get near it. Later, in '90, '91 and '92, I often walked over the Down from Haslemere to paint, and made this and several other drawings of the cottage'.

A Cottage near Blackdown • *Helen Allingham*

Valewood Farm under Blackdown • *Helen Allingham*

The Clothes Line • *Helen Allingham*

Helen Allingham's work was greatly admired in her day and although she is now remembered as the supreme exponent of the cottage watercolour she was also a fine painter of portraits. Among her admirers was John Ruskin, the great art critic, social reformer and ardent champion of Turner and the Pre-Raphaelites. He exerted a strong, almost oppressive, influence over the artists of his day. He regarded Helen Allingham's portraits as a waste of her talent and told her husband: 'I am indeed sorrowfully compelled to express my regret that she should have spent unavailing pains in finishing single heads, which are at the best uninteresting miniatures, instead of fulfilling her true gift, and doing what the Lord made her for in representing the gesture, character, and humour of charming children in country landscapes.' The watercolour medium does not lend itself well to portraiture so it is quite an achievement that some of her portraits are among her finest works. He was critical of the above picture painted in 1879 complaining about the introduction of the red handkerchief saying that the colour jarred. At other times he could be effusive about her work almost to the point of absurdity. In his *Academy Notes* he wrote about one of her watercolours describing it as 'a thing which I believe Gainsborough would have given one of his pictures for, – old fashioned as red-tipped daisies are – and more precious than rubies'. His poetic approach reached new heights when he wrote, 'The radiance and innocence of reinstated infant divinity showered again among the flowers of the English meadows of Mrs Allingham.' The picture on the left shows Valewood Farm, a medieval cottage which Helen Allingham would have passed many times on her visits to her friends, the Mangles, who lived further up the road at Valewood House. James Mangles was a friend of Alfred, Lord Tennyson and a world authority on rhododendrons.

A Cottage near Brook, Witley, Surrey • *Helen Allingham*

Both these watercolours are of Witley, which is situated between Godalming and Haslemere in west Surrey, and which became a centre for artists and writers, especially those interested in the cottage and country life. Many wanted to escape from the grey smog of London and by spending part of their time in Surrey they became prototype 'commuters'. The improvement in rail links meant that Witley was easily accessible and its unspoiled, rural beauty exerted a magnetic attraction. George Eliot who lived at The Heights wrote about the area describing it as 'a land of pine woods and copses, village greens and heather-covered, with the most delicious old red or grey brick timbered cottages nestling among creeping roses.'

The Allinghams had left London for Witley in 1881 and moved to a house called Sandhills and it was from this base that she painted many of the local cottages such as the ones illustrated here. When they had to leave to go back to Hampstead in 1888 because of William Allingham's ill-health, the artist and writer, W. Graham Robertson and his mother, moved into their home. His reaction to Witley was one of wonderment as he admitted in his memoirs *Time Was*, 'The district was really rustic and unspoilt, ancient legends and beliefs still lingered . . . almost for the first time in my life I found myself living in the real English country.' In 1860, Myles Birket Foster rented Tigbourne Cottage, an idyllic refuge for the summer months. Later, he made Witley his permanent home when he built a large house there called The Hill on Wormley Hill, the interior decoration of which was contributed to by such luminaries as William Morris and Sir Edward Burne-Jones. Nearby lived the poet Alfred, Lord Tennyson at Aldworth who was a great friend of William Allingham, Helen Allingham's husband.

A Cottage near Witley, Surrey • *Helen Allingham*

Children Playing • *Myles Birket Foster*

The Faggot Gatherer • *Myles Birket Foster*

Myles Birket Foster was born in North Shields in 1825 but his family moved to London when he was five and he became an apprentice wood engraver by the age of sixteen. He earned his living as a line drawing artist for various magazines such as *The Illustrated London News* but in his thirties he started painting watercolours and was swiftly elected to the Royal Watercolour Society. When he died in 1899, a journalist commented on his watercolours in *The Daily Graphic* that 'they were carefully done and finely finished, they were never slovenly, but always conscientious and they were the sort of art people could understand . . .', an obituary which highlights the lasting appeal of his work. His pictures are, in short, a delightful evocation of cottage life at the end of the nineteenth century.

For Myles Birket Foster, unlike his contemporary Helen Allingham, the central focus of his watercolours is the people rather than the cottage and they are usually engaged in some sort of activity rather than standing idly by a cottage gate. Although many of his watercolours show an idealized interpretation of cottage life he was not afraid to paint run-down cottages and poverty. His work is instantly recognizable as much for the subject matter as for his use of bodycolour and for the stippled technique with which he applied it.

Outside the Cottage • *Myles Birket Foster*

Feeding Time • *Myles Birket Foster*

One of Myles Birket Foster's friends and neighbours in Surrey was the poet Alfred, Lord Tennyson who lived at Aldworth on Blackdown, which was not far from Birket Foster's home at Witley. Before buying Aldworth, Tennyson lived at Farringford at Freshwater on the Isle of Wight and it was here that Birket Foster was asked by Tennyson, 'Why do you painters always prefer a tumbledown cottage to others?' to which Birket Foster replied, 'Because no one likes an unbroken [line]!' On another occasion, as Arthur Paterson recalls in *The Homes of Tennyson* (1905), Tennyson turned to him and asked 'Why a new cottage would be called "unpaintable" when, if the same cottage became old, delapidated, and dirty, with a big hole in the roof, and a half-naked child sprawling over the doorstep, it would be called "picturesque"!'

The watercolours shown here illustrate Birket Foster's point that a tumbledown cottage makes a more interesting picture than a perfect one. He was perhaps subconsciously echoing the Picturesque theories of James Malton who in 1798 in his *Essay on British Cottage Architecture* stressed that cottages must, more than anything else, be 'irregular'. Indeed, a decade later Mrs Dashwood in Jane Austen's *Sense and Sensibility* (1811) scornfully notes: 'As a cottage it was defective, for the building was regular.'

On the Thames • *Myles Birket Foster*

Near Haslemere • *Helen Allingham*

The Society of Painters in Watercolours had its origins in the Old Watercolour Society founded in 1804 by artists such as William Sawrey Gilpin, who was the first President, and John Varley. The aim of the Society was to hold exhibitions devoted entirely to watercolours and demonstrate the importance of this peculiarly British school of painting. It was immensely popular and in 1881 it became the Royal Society of Painters in Watercolour. Two exhibitions were held annually, one in the Summer and one in the Winter, and Queen Victoria is known to have been a regular visitor. For watercolourists, it was considered the most important society as Myles Birket Foster concluded when he wrote to his brother soon after he had been elected an Associate in 1860: 'The Gallery at Pall Mall East is the best place to have watercolour drawings exhibited and it has been a great desire of mine to get into the Society that I might be enabled to send pictures there!' Birket Foster was elected a full member two years later in 1862. Originally, there had been resistance to his election, as many considered his extensive use of bodycolour contrary to the spirit of watercolour painting. However, he soon became a dominant member and exhibited three-hundred-and-ninety-seven works there. Helen Allingham was also a prolific exhibitor showing over four-hundred-and-twenty-three watercolours. She was elected an associate in 1875 and became the first woman to be elected a full member in 1890.

Sand Hole Lane • *Myles Birket Foster*

The Arrival of Hop Pickers, Farnham • *Myles Birket Foster*

The large number of pictures painted by artists working in the cottage genre reflects the enormous popularity that this type of painting enjoyed. The increase in wealth of the new middle-classes meant that there were many more people interested in buying art and the success of exhibitions of cottage paintings at commercial galleries, such as the Fine Art Society and Agnews in London, suggests that buyers living in the cities were eager to be reminded of the countryside.

The extent to which it was possible to make a living is testified by Helen Allingham whose husband died in 1889 leaving her two hundred guineas. Thirty years later, after having brought up three children, she died leaving sixteen thousand pounds, money she had made from selling her watercolours.

Myles Birket Foster who was even more commercially successful than Allingham died in 1899 leaving thirty thousand pounds, a substantial sum in those days and the picture above sold in 1890 for five hundred pounds.

In the watercolour on the left, the cottages at the top of the bank are, in fact, alms-houses. There were five of them and although their origins are obscure they are recorded as existing as early as 1767. After Birket Foster sold this painting for one hundred guineas, the lane was renamed One Hundred Guineas Lane. At one time the Godalming to Chichester road ran through it. Today, it is just a narrow footpath.

Selling White Mice • *Myles Birket Foster*

The technique used to create a watercolour is always complex and it varies enormously from artist to artist. Myles Birket Foster tended towards a stippled technique using a lot of bodycolour (watercolour pigment mixed with Chinese white) which earned him the disapproval of Ruskin, who wrote in his Art of England lectures at Oxford in 1883 that he disliked Birket Foster's 'mere spotty execution' which he believed denied him 'the high position that was open to him as an illustrator of rustic life'. Thomas Mackay on the other hand used thin watercolour washes on wet paper to give an almost blurred effect while Charles Edward Wilson would carefully apply the pigment which complemented his studied and detailed approach to his subject matter. A good description of how Helen Allingham used the watercolour medium is given by Marcus B. Huish in his book *The Happy England of Helen Allingham* (1903), when he wrote how she obtained effects by 'rubbing, scrubbing and scratching . . . Now nowhere are these methods of Mrs. Allingham's more utilised, and with greater effect, than in her drawings of flower-gardens . . . The plan adopted a generation or so ago was first to draw and paint the flowers and then the foliage. This method left the flowers isolated objects and the foliage without substantiality . . . [Allingham's flowers are] carved out of a background . . . and left as white paper, all their drawing and modelling being achieved by a dextrous use of the knife and a wetted and rubbed surface . . . There are no badly pencilled outlines, and the blooms blend amongst themselves and grow naturally out of their foliage'.

The difference in technique is well illustrated by comparing the stippled technique of the Myles Birket Foster watercolour on the left with that of Helen Allingham's on the right.

By the Garden Wall • *Helen Allingham*

A Moment's Rest • *Carlton Alfred Smith*

Carlton Alfred Smith was born in 1853, the son of a steel engraver, and was educated in France before joining the Slade School of Art in London. He began his career as a lithographer before becoming a highly successful watercolourist who exhibited many times at the Royal Academy. He was a friend of Charles Edward Wilson, who he encouraged to become a professional painter, and at one time they shared a studio at Smith's house in Haverstock Hill near Hampstead. Later, he and his family went to live in Witley in Surrey to join the already flourishing artistic community there headed by Myles Birket Foster and Helen Allingham. They leased Vine Cottage and stayed there for ten years. It is from here that he painted many of the watercolours for which he is so well known.

For Smith, the focus of his pictures is the figure depicted either in a cottage interior or by the side of a cottage. He was a very talented draughtsman and his watercolours show a good understanding of light and colour. In many of his pictures, he uses the same models and among his favourites were his wife and two young daughters, one of whom on account of her short cropped hair was also painted as a young boy. The picture on the right shows a young girl holding an orange, something which was considered a great luxury at this time and was only eaten on special occasions. The picture on the left of a young woman staring directly at the viewer has the stillness and timelessness of a Dutch seventeenth-century picture.

The Birthday Book • *Carlton Alfred Smith*

Playing with the Kitten • *Charles Edward Wilson*

Like Helen Allingham and Myles Birket Foster, Charles Edward Wilson lived near Witley and drew inspiration from the surrounding countryside and the rustic way of life. His roots, however, were very different having been brought up in the heart of the industrial city Sheffield, where from the precocious age of eight he took art lessons at the Arundel Street School of Art. He found employment first of all as an industrial designer and later, as an illustrator for a French magazine called *L'Art*, which resulted in him travelling extensively across Europe.

Wilson's real wish had always been to become a professional watercolourist and in 1891 he exhibited at the Royal Academy for the first time. In 1895, after sharing a studio with his friend and early mentor Carlton Alfred Smith, Wilson found a large heather-thatched barn at Milford Common near Godalming which he used both as his studio and home.

Wilson adored the simple way of life in the country and Surrey at this time was still considered unspoilt, although a neighbour of his, Gertrude Jekyll, was expressing her concerns about the spread of urbanization and the increase of commuters in to west Surrey. In his pictures he used local children and farmworkers as his models and quite often the same model appears in a number of different pictures. Among his favourites were a Mrs Collins and her son Cecil. It is also said that the magpie, which so frequently appears in his pictures, was reared by him and after it died he had it stuffed by a taxidermist so he could continue to paint it! He also used old smocks and bonnets for his models even though they had gone out of fashion several decades earlier. Perhaps his greatest strength as a watercolourist was the way in which he could create the atmosphere of a cottage interior with careful attention to detail and a subtle use of colour and light.

The Bird's Nest • *Charles Edward Wilson*

Near Pulloxhill, Bedfordshire • *Henry John Sylvester Stannard*

Henry John Sylvester Stannard's watercolours epitomize our idea of an idyllic Victorian cottage world where the abundant hollyhocks and colourful lupins are not ruffled by a breath of wind. To a great extent, in both content and technique, he is an amalgam of both Myles Birket Foster and Helen Allingham but, unlike them, his world is less complex and his pictures are in many ways a straightforward exercise in nostalgia.

Stannard came from a large and successful family of artists, the most well-known being Lilian, Theresa, Alexander and Emily. He was born in London in 1870 and educated in Bedford, where he spent most of his life. His father, Henry Stannard, was a sporting artist and encouraged his son to paint from an early age; he exhibited his first picture, *A Note on the Ouse*, at the Royal Society of British Artists, and was elected a member in 1909.

In 1905 he received permission from Queen Alexandra to work at Sandringham, and spent much time painting the Queen's gardens and woods. She became so enthusiastic about Stannard's garden scenes that she bought more than twenty of his pictures. Royal patronage also came from abroad; in 1909 Marie Louise of Schleswig-Holstein bought one of his works. Such patronage led the *Arts Review* in 1908 to describe Stannard as 'one of the best-known English artists of our time', and soon many of his works were being used to illustrate books or were made into prints.

Children Playing by a Cottage • *Henry John Sylvester Stannard*

Old Cottage at Alcomb, Somerset • *Arthur Claude Strachan*

Surprisingly very few biographical details are known about Arthur Claude Strachan, the painter of these two delightful pictures. He was born in 1865 in Edinburgh and studied in Liverpool where he spent much of his life. He also lived in Warwick, Evesham and Glasgow. His work was much in demand during his lifetime and he exhibited at the Royal Academy and the Royal Institute of Painters in Watercolours. His pictures are unashamedly nostalgic and sentimental and his subject matter varies little from depicting children standing outside a cottage on a summer's day. He was one of the second generation of cottage painters and was influenced by both Helen Allingham and Myles Birket Foster. His work is usually very technically accomplished but can vary in quality; at his best he shows a good understanding of colour, light and texture. He travelled widely in England and worked in a number of counties including Worcestershire, Somerset, Cheshire and Oxfordshire.

Feeding Ducks • *Arthur Claude Strachan*

Buttercups • *Caroline Paterson*

No-one could be blamed for thinking that this delightful watercolour above is by Helen Allingham. In fact, it is by her sister Caroline Paterson who was a most accomplished artist. She too started her career as an illustrator of children's books and both her palette and technique are very similar to her sister's and their early watercolours are often confused as both artists signed Paterson. It was only after Helen married the poet William Allingham and Caroline married the etcher Sutton Sharpe in 1892, that their signatures prevented any further confusion. Unfortunately, Caroline's reputation as an artist has always been eclipsed by her more well-known sister.

Fred Walker, the artist of the picture on the right, was enormously talented and he influenced a whole generation of artists, especially Myles Birket Foster, but his career was cut short by ill-health and tragically he died at the early age of thirty-five, having contracted consumption. He was strongly influenced by the Pre-Raphaelites and this can be seen in this picture by both his palette and his careful attention to domestic detail. For instance, note the foreshortened watering can sitting on the large water barrel, the plate rack inside the door and the meticulously painted pea pods. He rather enigmatically said of this woman shelling peas, 'I meant her to be a little *creamy* sort of woman'.

The Housewife • *Frederick Walker*

ACKNOWLEDGEMENTS

I would like to thank the many people who have been so generous with both their time and help. In particular, I am greatly indebted to Annabel Watts who kindly read the manuscript and gave some excellent advice and made a number of pertinent suggestions. My thanks are also due to Emma Way of Weidenfeld and Nicolson who encouraged me to do the book and to my editor Suzannah Gough who has guided the project with great skill and professionalism. I would also like to thank Georgina Pope of Christie's, Sarah Colgrave of Sotheby's, Margarita Crutchley of Christie's Images, Caroline Oliphant of Bonhams, Diana Kay of Phillips, Ina Taylor, Chris Beetles, David James, Ruth Guthrie, Ric James, Brenda Tew, Danny Kinahan and the ever helpful staff of the London Library. Finally, I would like to thank my wife for her enthusiasm, patience and support.

Illustration Acknowledgements

The illustrations in this book have been reproduced by kind permission of the following:

CHRIS BEETLES LTD, ST JAMES'S, LONDON pp. 50, 60, 65
BONHAM'S p. 81
BOURNE GALLERY pp. back cover, 48
CHRISTIE'S pp. half-title, contents, 6, 11, 14, 19, 22, 27, 30, 34, 35, 36, 38, 39, 41, 53, 54, 67, 78, 79, 80, 84, 85, 89, 90, 91, 94, 99, 102, 111, 113, 114, 119, 122, 123, 125, 126, 127, 128, 130, 131, 134, 135, 140, 141, 144, 146, 147, 152
FINE ART PHOTOGRAPHS & LIBRARY LTD p. 143
FINE-LINES FINE ART p. 108
GALLERY FIVE p. 23
RICHARD GREEN GALLERY pp. 25, 28, 72, 83, 88, 96, 101, 136
RICHARD HAGEN LTD p. 100
HAMPTONS FINE ART p. 98
DAVID JAMES pp. 26, 33, 46, 58, 74, 87, 105, 106, 148, 150
LAWRENCE FINE ART, CREWKERNE p. 56
THE LEGER GALLERIES LTD p. 86
PHILLIPS pp. 29, 77
POLAK GALLERY pp. 57, 75
PRIORY GALLERY pp. front cover, 37, 42, 76, 132
PRIVATE COLLECTION pp. 59, 71, 82, 124, 129, 133, 154, 158
SOTHEBY'S pp. 24, 31, 32, 40, 43, 44, 45, 47, 49, 51, 52, 55, 61, 70, 93, 95, 97, 104, 107, 109, 110, 112, 137, 138, 139, 145, 149, 151, 153
THE TATE GALLERY pp. 142, 155
COURTESY OF THE BOARD OF TRUSTEES OF THE V & A pp. title, 73, 92, 103
WATFORD BOROUGH COUNCIL, WATFORD MUSEUM COLLECTION p. 62

FURTHER READING

Baldry, A. L., *The Practice of Watercolour Painting*, 1911

Calthrop, Dion Clayton, *The Charm of the English Garden*, 1910, (Adam and Charles Black)

Clayton-Payne, Andrew and Elliott, Brent, *Victorian Flower Gardens*, 1988, (Weidenfeld and Nicolson)

Cundall, H. M., *Birket Foster*, 1906, (Adam and Charles Black)

Dick, Stewart, *The Cottage Homes of England*, 1909, (Edward Arnold)

Ditchfield, P. H., *The Cottages and the Village Life of Rural England*, 1912, (J. M. Dent)

Evans, Tony and Lycett Green, Candida, *English Cottages*, 1982, (Weidenfeld and Nicolson)

Hardie, Martin, *Watercolour Painting in Britain, Vol. III, The Victorian Period*, 1968, (B. T. Batsford)

Heath, Richard, *The Victorian Peasant*, 1989, (Alan Sutton Publishing)

Huish, Marcus B., *The Happy England of Helen Allingham*, 1903, (Adam and Charles Black)

Jekyll, Gertrude, *Old English Household Life*, 1925, (B. T. Batsford)

Jekyll, Gertrude, *Old West Surrey*, 1904, (Longmans, Green and Co.)

Jones, Sydney R., *English Village Homes and Country Buildings*, 1936, (B. T. Batsford)

Kilvert, Reverend Francis, *Diary 1870–1879*, 1977, (Penguin Books)

Lander, Hugh and Rauter, Peter, *English Cottage Interiors*, 1989, (Weidenfeld and Nicolson)

Lester, Anthony, *The Stannards of Bedfordshire*, 1984, (Eastbourne Fine Art)

Loudon, J. C., *Encyclopaedia of Cottage Architecture*, 1836

Marsh, Jan, *Back to the Land*, 1982 (Quartet Books Ltd)

Newall, Christopher, *Victorian Watercolours*, 1987, (Phaidon Press Ltd)

Paterson, Arthur, *The Homes of Tennyson*, 1905, (Adam and Charles Black)

Pocock, W. F., *Architectural Designs for Rustic Cottages and Picturesque Dwellings*, 1807

Price, Uvedale, *Essay on the Picturesque*, 1794

Quiney, Anthony, *The Traditional Buildings of England*, 1990, (Thames and Hudson)

Reynolds, Jan, *Birket Foster*, 1984, (Batsford)

Robertson, W. Graham, *Time Was*, 1931, (Hamish Hamilton)

Ruskin, John, *The Art of England*, (lectures given in Oxford), 1883, (George Allan)

Samuel, Raphael, *Village Life and Labour*, 1975, (Routledge and Kegan Paul)

Spielmann, M. H. and Layard, G. S. *Kate Greenaway*, 1905, (Adam and Charles Black)

Taylor, Ina, *Helen Allingham's England, An Idyllic Rural View*, 1990, (Webb and Bower)

Thompson, Flora, *Lark Rise to Candleford*, 1973 (Penguin Modern Classics)

Weaver, Lawrence, *The 'Country Life' Book of Cottages*, 1913, (Country Life Books)

Wood, Christopher, *Dictionary of Victorian Painters*, 1978, (Antique Collectors Club)

Woodforde, John, *The Truth about Cottages*, 1979, (Routledge and Kegan Paul)

Vine Cottage • *Helen Allingham*

INDEX

Page numbers in *italics* refer to illustrations